THE
INTERNATIONAL
BOOK OF
WINES

HAMLYN London New York Sydney Toronto

THE INTERNATIONAL BOOK OF WINES

Published by
The Hamlyn Publishing Group Limited
London · New York · Sydney · Toronto
Astronaut House, Feltham, Middlesex, England
© Copyright The Hamlyn Publishing Group Limited 1975

ISBN 0 600 31334 4

Phototypeset by Tradespools Ltd, Frome, Somerset
Printed in The Canary Islands (Spain) by
Litografía A. Romero, S.A.
Santa Cruz de Tenerife
D. L. TF. 820 - 1975

Maps drawn by David Mostyn
Line drawings by Graham Beehag

Contents

Wines & Spirits

There is nothing at all daunting about wines and spirits. Some people are shy of them, and of wines especially, because they feel that unless they have an extensive knowledge of them they are going to make some dreadful gaffe and appear socially graceless and unworldly. There are more nervous tremors at the approach of the wine waiter than there are over the approach of the bill.

Wines, and to a lesser extent spirits, are certainly a complex subject, but few people outside the wine and spirit business have an exhaustive knowledge of them, and even in the wine and spirit business there is a tendency to specialise, so that the man who knows the A to Z of the Rhineland may well be lost among Burgundies. Nor is it in any way necessary to possess a comprehensive knowledge of wine in order to enjoy it. Wine is for drinking, drinking is for pleasure. The only essentials are that you should know what you like, and be able to ensure that you get what you like.

Stripped of its dignity, wine is almost starkly simple: fermented grape juice. Fermentation transforms the sugar in the juice into ethyl alcohol and carbon dioxide.

Red wine is made by gently crushing red grapes, which have usually been stripped off their stalks, and fermenting the resulting juice or 'must' along with the skins, pulp and pips. The pips and skins produce tannin to give the wine body and staying power, while the skins give the wine its colour.

White wine can be made from white or red grapes. The juice is separated from the skins and other solid matter straightaway after pressing, and therefore takes on no colour.

Rosé wine is a halfway house between these two methods. The juice of red grapes is allowed to remain in contact with the skins and pips for some time after pressing – perhaps for a matter of hours only, depending on the maker's formula. The juice takes on sufficient colour from the skins to give it the delightfully fresh hue associated with rosé.

Sparkling wines may be red, white or rosé. They begin life as still, dry wines made by any of the above methods. Then a predetermined quantity of sugar is added to make the fermentation start again, and the wine is enclosed in bottles (in the case of the Champagne method) or in tanks (the *cuve close* method). This secondary fermentation fills the wine with bubbles of carbon dioxide gas which, since they are held captive, marry with the wine to make sparkling wine.

Fortified wines also start as ordinary still wines. Fortification is simply the addition of brandy; the addition may be made either while the wine is fermenting or afterwards. If it is added during fermentation the fermentation will stop, and since not all the sugar in the grape juice will have been converted into alcohol, the end-product will be a sweet wine. In the case of sherry, brandy is added simply to increase the strength of the wine; in the case of port, it is added expressly to stop the fermentation.

Spirits are no more mysterious. Anything that is fermentable can form their base: grapes, in the case of brandy, grain, in the case of whisky, molasses, in the case of rum, and so on. Once fermentation has taken place the resulting alcoholic liquid is distilled. This process is based on the fact that alcohol, because it is lighter than water, will vaporise at a lower temperature, so that when a liquid with some alcohol in it is heated to a temperature between the boiling point of the two, the rising vapours can be collected and condensed to form a liquid of greater alcoholic strength.

Another stage of distillation is rectification, in which the distillate is redistilled to purify it further. At the same time its alcoholic strength is increased.

There are two kinds of still: the pot still, which involves a somewhat laborious process, used for malt whisky, brandy and some kinds of rum; and the patent still, a much more productive apparatus used for grain whisky, vodka and gin.

This, in elementary terms, is what wines and spirits are. If they were as simple and straightforward as this, there would be little more to say. But every kind of wine and spirit has its separate personality, deriving from a range of factors, such as where it is made, by what method, and from what raw material. These elements in the make-up of alcoholic beverages all add up to its total individuality.

Grapes are the raw material of wine of all kinds, but they are not, clearly, any kind of grapes grown anywhere. There are certain classic grapes used in wine-making. Cabernet Sauvignon is the great red wine grape of Bordeaux. Pinot Noir makes the most magnificent wines of Burgundy, and is also the principal grape of the Champagne area. Chardonnay is the foremost grape in the white wine-producing district of Burgundy. Riesling is the famous grape of the Rhine and Moselle. Furmint produces the rich golden wine of Tokay.

There are countless more grape varieties, some as famous as these, others obscure. The best of the European varieties are cultivated all over the wine-growing world, and many of the 'newer' wine-producing countries – Australia, South Africa and the United States, for example – make wine from such grapes as the Riesling, the Pinot Noir and the Cabernet with excellent results.

In the nineteenth century, the wine industry of Europe came close to extinction with the arrival of the phylloxera from America. This burrowing parasite, a native of North America, arrived in Europe in the 1860s and within the next quarter of a century had decimated the vineyards of Europe. It would have been the end of the road for wine in Europe had it not been discovered, in the nick of time, that native American vines are immune to the bug. The remedy was obvious: cuttings of the classic European vines had to be grafted on to American roots. The remedy was a success, and the wine-growers breathed again, though it was to take a long time for the industry to recover fully from the disaster. Here and there a few pockets of vines did not succumb to the scourge, but they are rare exceptions. Today the great majority of European vines are still grafted on to American roots.

Vines, of course, bear fruit every year, and every year there is a vintage. But, rather perplexingly, every year is not a *vintage* year. In Champagne and in the port wine district in the Douro valley, for example, the makers declare a vintage, and put a date on the bottle, only when they consider that the wine of that year is outstandingly good. Otherwise they blend the wine of one year with that of others. Champagne that is so made is known as NV (non-vintage).

There are, again, other areas where the year in which a wine was made is more or less immaterial, for the wine of one year is so much like that of another. In the case of such wines, from areas which have a constant climate, the vintage date on the bottle is important only as an indication of how mature the wine is.

But for growers in the areas that produce the world's most prized wines, notably France and Germany, life is a lot less certain. Winter frost can kill the dormant vines. Summer hail can wipe out the crop. Too much or too little sun or rain can in a very short period change the promise of a fine year into the certainty of a poor one. All vineyards in countries with variable weather face the same risk.

It would simplify matters, for the consumer if for no-one else, if there were just good years and bad years. But there are years that are above average and years that are below average. There are 'mixed' years, when localities in a single area can produce worthy wine while the near-neighbours simply can't make the grade. And there are years when the wine is initially rated as indifferent after the early sampling but which proves, when it has attained some maturity, to be better than average. The reverse can also happen.

Nothing can be taken for granted. Even the vintage charts which are published, with ratings for complete wine-producing areas, can mislead because there are always some, if not many, exceptions to the general rule. All the same, provided one recognises their limitations, such charts can give useful guidance of a generalised kind.

But the consumer's best friend ought to be his wine merchant, and if he is not, the consumer should shop elsewhere. The merchant will (or should) give an objective opinion on his own vintages.

Not a few people mistakenly hold all old wine in high esteem. But old wine is not necessarily good wine, and even an outstanding vintage can fade if it is kept too long. It may not, in such a condition, be wholly undrinkable, but it might have been better had it been opened a few years sooner.

And, again contrary to widespread belief, much wine will not improve at all by being left to rest in bottle after being drawn from the cask. This applies to most dry whites, which are made to drink young, while they are fresh and flowery, but which are likely to lose these attributes and become jaded if they are kept for a lengthy period in bottle. The same applies to light reds which, far from improving if left in bottle indefinitely, will actually deteriorate.

The wines that will improve in bottle over a period of several years are the best and better qualities of red wine – claret, Burgundy, some Italian wines and port are examples. A few whites will also show an improvement. They are mostly the luscious sweet whites – Sauternes and the rich Rhine and Moselle wines made from late-gathered grapes. And some of the exceptional dry whites from Burgundy can also develop in character during a prolonged stay in the bottle.

There is much confusion over aged spirits, and especially over brandy. From time to time people advertise inviting offers for a bottle of, say, century-old brandy. But if that brandy has been in the bottle for 100 years, then it will be no different now from the time it first went into it. Spirits do not improve in bottle, only in cask. It is even possible that the brandy will be *worse* than it was when it was bottled, if the cork has begun to dissolve into the spirit.

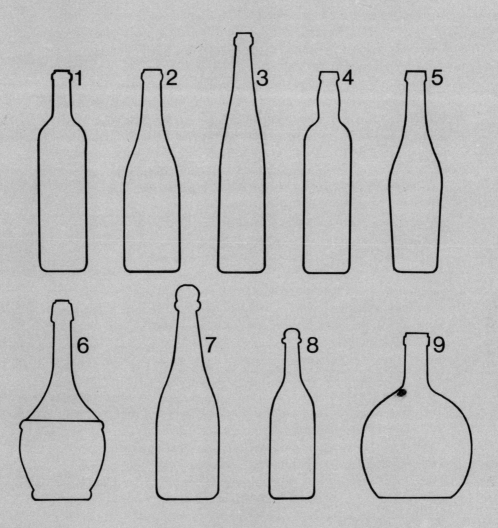

1 Square-shouldered Bordeaux bottle, green for red wine and clear for white; 2 Burgundy bottle with more sloping sides, dark green for red and white; 3 Tall slender classic German bottle, green for Moselle and brown for Rhine wines – the Alsatian version is slightly taller but holds the same amount; 4 Vintage port bottle; 5 Beaujolais 'pot' containing ½ litre; 6 Traditional Chianti flask in its plaited straw cover; 7 and 8 Champagne bottle and half bottle; 9 Franconian Bocksbeutel, used for Steinwein

Everyone has heard of fine wine. Within the context of table wines generally, the word fine has no formal definition, and it is not even a term with a meaning unanimously agreed among wine drinkers, let alone wine-makers. Indeed, anyone can call his wine fine (unless there is a law against it, which there is in some countries). He can even call it finest, or some other superlative. I have seen a bottle in Portugal which described itself as 'the greatest of the finest'.

But fine wine, in the accepted sense, is the best quality of Bordeaux and Burgundy, the Rhine and the Moselle. Tokay, from Hungary, is undoubtedly another. Some would argue as to whether good-quality Italian wine, like the best kinds of Chianti, are fine wines; but if there were ever to be a formal classification of the world's wines, such wines should certainly have a place in the upper echelons. And there are numerous other candidates, not least from countries which do not necessarily have a long wine tradition.

Even with the most broad and generous of definitions, however, fine wines represent only a minute drop of the world's total wine output. Beneath the small number of top qualities there is an immense range of plainer wines, from those that have some of the attributes of fine wines down to uncomplicated blends for everyday drinking.

There is a widespread impression that there is something not quite legitimate, possibly even sinister, about blending wines. But blending is perfectly allowable for most wines (provided they do not claim to be something other than blends). Blending is the rule rather than the exception in Champagne. It is the basis of the solera system by which sherry is made. The popular varieties of Rhine and Moselle wines are blends. In Burgundy, with vineyards divided into innumerable small parcels each tended by its individual owner with his own ideas about how to run a vineyard, some wines have to be blends, otherwise they would be uncommercial.

The blended wine from France and Germany that is most familiar in the United Kingdom is the everyday branded bottle. The range of price and quality is considerable, but most set out to be honest, straight-forward wines at a reasonable cost. Few of them have a vintage year on the label, for the object of making up these blends is to create something that has, so far as possible, universal appeal, and will remain constant from one year to another. Having found its public it does not vary except in minor respects which are likely to be discernible only to the blender himself.

The least expensive of these wines are often sold in export markets as *vin ordinaire*. They are, in fact, a long way from the basic vin ordinaire of France; that can be ghastly – tarry, gritty, and utterly unlovable. It stains your lips, leaves your mouth sanded and, later, your head splitting.

But this is authentic, earthy ordinaire. You are unlikely to find it outside its place of origin. The man in the black beret, swigging from a bottle under a hedgerow anywhere in France, knows it and is used to it and buys it on no more selective a basis than its alcoholic strength. The ordinaires that are sold abroad are of a considerably more refined sort. They are carefully made and have a measure of style about them. Certainly they are not to be despised, for they provide the opportunity to drink wine regularly, a pleasure that is probably denied on economic grounds to those who insist that any wine should be 'fine' or even 'good'.

Back up at the top of the scale again there are a number of wines that cause bafflement by describing themselves as 'château-bottled', 'domaine-bottled' or 'estate-bottled', or the corresponding words in the language of their country of origin. They sometimes cause not only bafflement but irritation, for in general they cost more than wines that do not make the same boast.

Château-bottling is a guarantee of authenticity. The earning power of any strip of vine-bearing land is closely related to how the world at large rates its end-product; the grower takes no chances with his methods of viticulture and vinification. The nightmare is that someone else might try to turn a quick penny by counterfeiting the result of the grower's work. If the wine is tampered with – diluted, adulterated, or simply faked – the reputation of the vineyard declines and so does the long-term market value of its wine. It is too easy for a dishonest middleman to buy a few casks of some meritorious wine and multiply its volume simply by tipping in a few casks of something cheaper. That is why château-bottling began.

Bottling his own wine, using a branded cork, the grower implies a guarantee that the wine is genuinely his product. Sometimes he even numbers the bottles to make extra sure. The practice started in Bordeaux: *mis* (or *mise*) *en bouteilles au château* is the form of words on the label.

The cost of small-scale bottling, as well as the extra freight charges for shipping wine in bottle-units instead of in bulk, adds to the ultimate price of the wine. There are some instances where it is not worth paying this extra money because, as château- and estate-bottling has grown from its original status as a guarantee into a distinction with a commercial value, the growers of some rather indifferent wines in Europe and elsewhere have climbed aboard the bandwagon in the hope that their produce will fetch a better price.

There are established understandings about the use of wine denominations. There are established misunderstandings, too, not to mention established disagreements. All this gives rise to a great deal of confusion.

Thus one British wine merchant, in an advertisement headed 'port', was not long ago offering a South African dessert wine with the recommendation that restaurateurs could stock it as a 'house' port. The merchant deserved, and may well have had, a stiff note from the port wine shippers, for British law recognises that port comes only from Portugal. Any restaurateur who took the merchant's advice would probably be in even hotter water. Fortified dessert wines from South Africa, Australia, or elsewhere may call themselves more or less what they please in the United Kingdom, but never port or anything suggestive of a Portuguese origin. The most common name for such wines is ruby.

Sherry, on the other hand, enjoys no such protection, and anyone may call his wine sherry with impunity. Plenty do, in South Africa, Australia, Cyprus, California and elsewhere. This free usage has become so established that it would be pedantic to argue that the word sherry should be reserved exclusively for the original Spanish product. But it would be hard to find anyone in Jerez, the home of Spanish sherry, and the place name from which the wine name derives, to agree with that view.

The practice of 'borrowing' the names of classic European wines and affixing them to wines made elsewhere in Europe or elsewhere in the world is one of the biggest bones of contention in the wine business. French place names are the most abused. Producers of sparkling wine in various countries unashamedly call their product Champagne. Australian wine growers are among those who may describe any full-bodied red as Burgundy. In California they label certain sweet wines Sauternes (and not infrequently Sauterne) in defiance of the Gallic sensitivities of the growers of that great district of France. Wines of foreign origin bearing such names are not permitted to enter France.

The world at large knows about these practices and is probably not deceived by name-borrowing. The victims, however, argue strongly that such names as Burgundy are debased by association with inferior wines made in other countries and that the consumer, having encountered an unpleasant non-Burgundian Burgundy, will form an ill opinion of *all* wines labelled Burgundy, including the authentic stuff.

The difficulty is that the practice is so well entrenched it is going to be hard to break it down. But a start has been made; instead of trying to identify the general style of a wine for the customer by the use of words like 'Sauternes' and 'Burgundy', more shippers are describing such wines as 'sweet white wine' or 'full-bodied red'. It's so simple you might wonder why they hadn't thought of it in the first place.

Another move away from dependence on European place names is the growing practice of describing wines by the name of the grape variety used to make them: thus Chilean Cabernet, Hungarian Riesling, and Californian Cabernet Sauvignon, among others.

One significant change affecting denominations on the British market has followed British admission to the European Economic Community. Membership requires compliance with the wine laws of the EEC countries, with the result that British labelling regulations, never previously subject to these rules, must now reflect their implications.

The most important consequence of this arises from the French Appellation Contrôlée (AC) laws, which stipulate, among other things, the *maximum* quantity an individual vineyard may produce per hectare (2·47 acres). The reasoning behind this rule was that, in general, the more wine a hectare of vines produces, the lower the quality of that wine is likely to be.

For years, however, and particularly in good vintages, many vineyards have produced more than their maximum yield as laid down by law. This surplus is not entitled to an AC certificate, and much of it was sold to British merchants who openly and lawfully sold it on their home market under parish or district names such as Nuits-Saint-Georges and Saint-Emilion – appellations which could be affixed only to AC certificated wines in France. The surplus, moreover, fetched a lower price than the certificated wine, with the result that the British were able for many years to drink quality French wines at a lower cost than the French themselves were obliged to pay.

Since 1973 French wine entering Britain has had to be accompanied by identifying documents, and although a period of harmonisation will allow stocks of vintage wines lying in Britain to be sold even though their documentation is non-existent, uncertificated wines bearing controlled names will before long be a memory.

All this, however, was anticipated by British merchants long before Britain's entry to the EEC, and a great new range of brand names appeared in readiness. Messrs. Smith and Company's Châteauneuf-du-Pape became their Châteauneuf-du-Pape 'Par Excellence'; now the district name has gone, although the wine still comes from there, and 'Par Excellence' and a multitude of like names, having established a following, continue to represent the same value for money and quality that their buyers have become accustomed to over the years.

Selecting & Serving Wine

BEAUNE

There are those who can't face red wine at any price, and drink white with beefsteak, baked ham or bombe surprise, come what may. Others again can't stand dry wine at all, and are happy with sweet or sweetish wines with savoury dishes.

There is nothing in the slightest bit dreadful about such deviations. A good, well-flavoured white wine can be on the most amiable of terms with many, if not all, of the meat dishes that are conventionally paired with reds, while fairly sweet wines, notably many of those made from the Riesling grape, are commonly served with savoury dishes. The Victorians and Edwardians regularly drank the great sweet wines of Bordeaux with the fish course: no wine waiter ever looked down his nose at them for it.

So the 'rules' about wine – what to drink with what, serving, storing, proper glasses, and so forth – are by no means inflexible, and it is not in any way a social outrage or a mark of unworldliness to adapt them to one's own preferences, or to ignore some of them altogether. And the rules, of course, are not rules at all; they are guidelines, crystallised from the world's experience of wine and food, and they are there to help, not to hinder, enjoyment.

There are certainly those who make too much fuss of wine. They have fixed ideas about right and wrong in the matter of wine. For them, the guidelines *are* rules, and the man who does not do his wine drinking by the book is a barbarian. Such people have an exaggerated respect for wine, and not infrequently for their own knowledge of it.

There are others who, however well-meaning, are much too dogmatic in their views on wine guidelines. A French writer, for example, in a booklet which is intended to *help* people to enjoy wine, observes: 'It is a heresy to serve fortified wines at the beginning of a meal . . . they make it impossible to appreciate the quality of wines such as Bordeaux, Burgundy, etc., which are served after them.'

Heresy is an incongruous word to use in the context of matching wine with food, but setting that aside, the statement will surprise those who have enjoyed dry Madeira or sherry with consommé, or white port with melon. In any case the French themselves have an improbable weakness for sweet, strongly flavoured aperitifs, which has extended, in recent years, to embrace ruby port, of all things. Maybe they have taken to rinsing their mouths out before sitting down to the first course.

At the other end of the scale there are those who make a boast of not merely ignoring the guidelines but despising them. Their view is that wine is no more than a commodity like beer or lemonade. They make no fuss over wine; they go to the other extreme, spurning decent glasses, rejecting decanting as an unnecessary frill, and sloshing handsome wines about in a way that would cause the maker to shudder if he could see it happening.

In between the fussers, the pedants and the anti-fussers are all those who are happy to acknowledge that the guidelines are helpful, if applied sensibly. Choose wine with care, serve it with consideration, and you will get the best from it.

Buying wine Choose a real wine merchant. Small wine-and-food stores may well have the expertise to purchase and handle wine properly, but sometimes they do not. It may be that there is inadequate storage space, so the bottles are kept standing upright; this can cause wine to go out of condition in a remarkably short space of time. Sometimes wines that have not been professionally handled can fade in flavour as well as in colour because they have been stored in a strong light. Wine is not fragile, but it does not have an infinite capacity for enduring ill-treatment either.

Going to an experienced, specialist merchant has the advantage of giving the customer a source of informed advice on his purchases. This does not make it any less important that the customer should have rather more than only the vaguest of notions of what he wants, and of how much he wants to spend. But a good merchant, if he is worth his salt, knows all his wines individually, and part of his training will have been to know how to advise the customer on how to spend his money sensibly, taking account of the customer's needs.

The best criterion for selecting wine for current drinking is the status of the occasion on which it is going to be served. There is no point in spending ninety per cent of the budget for a special dinner party on the food alone, leaving only enough to buy the humblest of wines. Inexpensive wines have their place at, for example, an informal supper party or at a lunch in the garden, but with well-prepared, expensive food such wines will show all their faults.

Before moving to more specific considerations in planning a meal, it should be said that wine buying ought not, whenever possible, to be a last-minute expedition. Most people, unless they have a cellar or a hoard of wine elsewhere in the house, buy wine as and when they need it. This may be convenient, but it does not help good wine, especially reds, which need time to recover after even a comparatively short journey. Buy the wine at least twenty-four hours in advance of the meal at which it is going to be served. In the case of a fine, aged red wine, buy a week in advance. Most reds, and some whites, with any bottle-age have sediment. This is swirled into the wine when the bottle is taken from the shop. Usually it needs no more than a few days in which to settle down.

Planning a meal If a dinner party is to be a special one, let the wine be as special as possible. A classed claret or a single-vineyard Burgundy is the kind of wine to aim for, provided, of course, that the central dish is of the kind that will accommodate such wines. If the central dish is fish, choose a stylish white Burgundy, Moselle, or dry Champagne.

A lavish dinner party may well be a two- or even three-wine occasion: a white with the fish course, red with the meat, and a dessert wine at the end. It is prudent to apportion most of the wine-budget to the main-course wine. An impeccable white Burgundy, like Corton-Charlemagne or Chassagne-Montrachet, will be magnificent with the fish course, but it will overshadow any following red wine that is not of comparable status. So unless all the wines served are from the top-drawer classics, which is an expensive way to entertain these days, the first and final course wines should be in supporting roles, the finest wine should be in the centre. Avoid serving a red with the first course if a white, however dignified, is to follow it.

Many of the considerations that apply to planning a dinner party also apply to planning a lunch, but unless the lunch is a formal one, no-one will expect, or want, more than one wine. Light reds and delicate whites fit into an informal lunch better than heavier flavours. They give the impression that, because they are light in body, they are also light in alcohol. This is by no means always the case in fact, but people, especially those with an afternoon's work ahead of them, like to feel they are having a relatively abstemious lunch, and if the wine at least seems low in alcohol, the chances are that they will feel much more relaxed. Rosé is good at a summer lunch with, say, cold chicken and ham.

A buffet lunch or supper is not usually a luxurious affair, so here there should be an opportunity to economise on the cost of wine – particularly since, on this kind of occasion, people tend to drink more than they would at a more formal occasion. A buffet that features, for example, cold game pie or fresh salmon salad deserves a wine of middle to good quality; one that features sandwiches, pâté, pork pies and so forth can get along very well with modest wines; such a meal, indeed, is one at which quantity, rather than quality, could be the right thing to aim for, using inexpensive blends.

Plain food does not, however, qualify only for the plainest kind of wine. One of the most economical ways to entertain is to offer a selection of cheeses with French loaves, accompanied by a well-bred red. Many varieties of cheese are, of course, expensive, but many of those are of the pungent variety that are not, in any case, best suited to serving with wine. Avoid those and choose a hard, mild cheese. The right wine and the right cheese will lift the status of the occasion from a snack meal to that of a repast.

The quantity of wine that should be allowed for each person on any kind of occasion is very much governed by how much money is in the kitty, and the quality of the wine chosen. An average wine bottle yields six good glasses; half a bottle per person is therefore quite liberal, and a glass-and-a-half or possibly two glasses of a fine wine at a stately lunch or dinner party, especially if there are supporting wines with other courses. At a buffet or picnic it may be prudent to allow rather more than three glasses a head – especially if the guests are pouring for themselves.

Appraising wine Having selected and bought your wine, make sure that it is in good condition before pouring it for your guests. This is important even if the wine is one with which you are familiar; it is still more important with a wine you have never before encountered.

Nothing is more certain to cast a pall of gloom over a dinner party than a wine that has 'gone off' in some way, or turns out to be unsuitable for the food it is to accompany.

An unfamiliar white or rosé can, for example, prove on tasting to be too sweet to be served with the dish it has been chosen for, notwithstanding the label's claim that it is dry or medium-dry. A red wine can prove to be too lightweight, or too heavy, for its chosen dish.

If a wine is wrong in this sort of way, one can elect to brazen it out with the guests, rather than consign the bottle to the kitchen sink. But a wine that is actually out of condition is a dead loss, unless the wine merchant can be persuaded to take it back.

Watch for cloudiness in the wine. This is best done by pouring a little into a glass and holding it against either a sunny window or artificial light. Cloudiness can simply mean that sediment has been disturbed, but this is not likely to be the case if the wine has been rested, and it has been handled gently. Wine should be bright. A cloudy one is almost certainly out of condition.

Cloudy or not, next sniff. Swirl the glass gently to release the aroma fully. A bad wine should leave you in no doubt about its state: it stinks. The cork may have shrunk and let the air get at the wine; in the case of a white wine the fault could be maderisation – a condition reached by wine kept over-long in the bottle. The first indication of this will be detected during the examination for cloudiness, for maderised wine turns an unnatural shade of brown.

Then there is that contentious condition, the bane of many a restaurateur and not a few wine merchants: corked wine. Such wine has been afflicted by mould from a deteriorating cork. The condition may be slight or chronic, but in either case the wine will be undrinkable.

Sometimes wine can smell of cork, but not unpleasantly so. Allow the bottle to stand for a short time. The chances are that the smell will go away and the wine will be perfectly pleasant. Another smell, in the case of some inexpensive white wines in which it is used as a preservative, is sulphur. There is nothing harmful about it and the smell should vanish in a few minutes.

Having scrutinised and sniffed the wine, the time has come to taste it. Roll the wine around your tongue and swallow. If it has passed the earlier tests it is unlikely that it will prove to be out of condition at this stage; tasting merely confirms that the wine is in good order. If it is not, tasting should reveal any defects frankly: a musty taste, a flavour of vinegar, and out it should go.

Decanting Pouring wine from a perfectly good bottle into another container looks, on the face of it, like one of the frills about wine-drinking that simply exasperate. But like choosing suitable glasses and serving at the right temperature, decanting does contribute to the maximum enjoyment of wine. If decanting were no more than merely a means of bringing the wine to the table in a container more presentable than its own bottle, it would be eminently expendable.

There are two purposes in decanting wine. The first, in the case of quality red wines and sometimes whites which have been in bottle for some years, is to leave the sediment in the bottle. The second is to aerate the wine.

Inexpensive, blended wines are made for immediate consumption and should have no sediment. In older wines the sediment will be lying at the base of the bottle if it has been removed from a wine bin

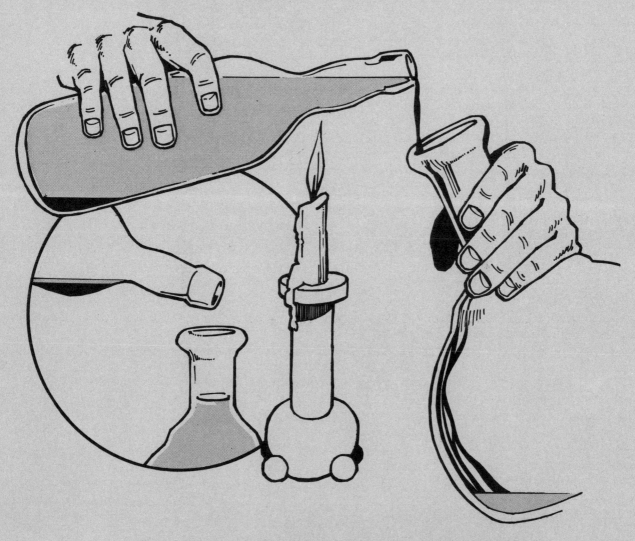

and has remained upright for several days, or in the case of a bottle that has been carefully removed from the wine bin and is to be decanted at once, it will be lying down much of one side of the bottle, which should be the reverse side from the label, or the main label, if there are two.

Decanting the bottle that has come straight from the bin needs the most care. Hold it against a reasonably strong light, so that the sediment is visible; if it is not visible at once it will become so as the bottle empties. Then pour, slowly and steadily, until the first of the sediment reaches the neck of the bottle. That is the time to stop, resisting the temptation to squeeze every last drop of unsedimented wine from the bottle at the risk of getting sediment in the decanter. Even a little sediment in the decanter will end up in someone's glass, and will taste muddy and disagreeable.

The wine in the decanter should be bright and clear. The small quantity that remains in the bottle with the sediment may be lamentable, but it can always be used, strained if necessary, for cooking.

Aeration is part of the decanting procedure. Wine and air are in most circumstances the worst of companions, but if air can get at the wine for a short time before it is to be drunk, the wine will get a breath of life it has not experienced since it went into the bottle. The result is an improvement in the wine that in many cases is remarkable.

All red wines benefit by this treatment, and the younger they are, the more they will benefit. However, red wine with considerable bottle age – more, say, than ten years – can fade in flavour quite quickly after

1 *Standard all-purpose wine glass;* 2 *Paris goblet ideal for red or white wine;* 3 *Tulip glass good for white and sparkling wines;* 4 *Traditional Champagne flûte;* 5 *Tall-stemmed glass traditional in Alsace and Germany;* 6 *Sherry glass or copita;* 7 *Brandy balloon*

only a short exposure to the air, so it is sensible to leave the decanting operation until ten minutes or so before it is due to be served.

The plainest of decanters will do. Avoid a jug, unless it has an exceptionally narrow top, for it is possible to over-aerate even comparatively youthful wines.

Glasses There is no need to invest in a variety of different kinds of wine glass. The conventional tinted glasses for hock, for example, were originally devised to conceal impurities in the wine, which are these days excluded by filtration and other modern methods in wine production. The Paris goblet, bulbous and stemmed, is the basic, all-purpose glass, and unless it is made of crystal, it is usually inexpensive. It comes in a range of sizes, the 2½-oz. (70-ml.) size being suitable for liqueurs, the 5-oz. (140-ml.) for port, sherry or brandy, and the 8-oz. (225-ml.) for table or sparkling wines.

However, standardisation of the type of glass you use can be tedious, particularly if you entertain regularly and serve a number of different drinks. Wine glasses can be fancier than simple Paris goblets, but they should be clear. Cut glass does not show off wine to the best advantage. Silver or stainless steel goblets are worse; they not only conceal the wine, but wine drunk from them can taste metallic.

Two other kinds of glass are worth acquiring for the sake of variety. The *flûte* glass – narrow where it joins the stem, widening up to the top – is the best glass for Champagne and other sparkling wines because it does not allow the bubbles to surface as readily as they will in a wide-topped glass, so the wine does not go flat quickly. 'Balloon' glasses, which are not unlike Paris goblets but curve in towards the top, help to capture the aroma of brandy, but they should be small. The immense balloons brought to the table in some restaurants allow, by their sheer size, the aroma to escape and, what is worse, the great expanse of glass the spirit must climb to reach the drinker's mouth retains not a little of the brandy; at the prices asked for brandy these days, why dispatch any of it to the dishwasher?

Serving Working out the right temperature at which to serve wine seems another of those irritating pieces of fussiness that drive people to beer. Who wants to carry around a thermometer to make sure a red is *chambré*, or a white cool but not chilled.

No need. Stand red wine, unopened, for four, twelve or twenty-four hours, as you wish, in the main, heated room of the house. It will then reach room temperature, the ideal temperature at which to serve most red wine. If you forget to do this, don't, at all costs, put it in the oven or under a hot tap, for no wine will be at its best if subjected to violent treatment. Rather pour it cool; in a warm dining room it should not take long, once poured into the glasses, to achieve an acceptable temperature.

Some light reds, like Beaujolais and Bardolino, can be served cool, especially in summer. Ideally this coolness should come from the coolest room of the house, rather than from the refrigerator, but in especially warm weather twenty minutes in the refrigerator is probably the best way of achieving the right degree of coolness.

Cold enhances the freshness of nearly all whites. They should not be frozen. The bottle should spend perhaps forty-five minutes in the refrigerator or twenty in a well-filled ice bucket. The objective is to bring down the temperature to the level it would have been at had the wine come from a cool cellar. This applies not only to white table wines but to dry or fairly dry sherry, Champagne and other sparkling wines.

At the table There is no special ceremony to observe in pouring wine. Simply pour the wine into the glasses and relax. The British are insistent that port should be passed to the left, the passer using his right hand to do so. Once your glass is empty it is taboo to reach for the decanter unless it is passed to you from the man on your right. It all adds up to nothing except that you should avoid sitting on the left of an absent-minded port-abstainer.

Wine remainders Resist the temptation to open more bottles than you will immediately need. Table wines will keep for only a short space of time once the cork has been withdrawn from the bottle, and sparkling wine will not keep at all unless the bottle is secured with one of the special clamps for that express purpose that are on the market these days.

Provided the bottle is firmly recorked, table wines should take no harm from being kept for about twenty-four hours. It is better to pour any remainders into an empty half bottle and cork that up firmly; in this way the wine will be good for several days. Remainders of old red wines must, regrettably, be disposed of, for they will turn to vinegar in only a matter of hours.

The heavier fortified wines, port, Madeira, sweet sherry, Marsala, and so forth, will not keep indefinitely. Make their maximum life-span three weeks after opening. Light sherries, fino and manzanilla, will keep for perhaps five days before they begin to wilt. Some people believe that vintage port is actually better if the bottle has been opened on the day before it is going to be consumed. Much depends on the age of the wine, but it is a risk that is better avoided with a late middle-aged or elderly wine.

Hangovers Sometimes they happen. Sometimes mixed drinks are made a good deal stronger than they ought to be. Sometimes an injudicious variety of drinks, even in comparatively small quantities, can have dire consequences. Sometimes, more simply and more frequently, you can have one, or two, or even three, too many.

There is a great rogues' gallery of hangover styles, but they all have one thing in common: all are disagreeable. It is happier not to dwell on such agonies. Prevention is better than cure.

Prevention, or avoidance, is essentially a matter of knowing your own capacity and staying within it – preferably below it. Downing drink for drink at a party is a convivial enough business, but no group of people can necessarily expect to have the same level of resistance to alcohol. You – or I – may be under the table before the others have even started to get under way.

If willpower is not enough (and alcohol can slacken willpower, just as it can reinforce it) then there are some elementary precautions to be taken at the start of a drink-risk occasion. A teaspoonful of olive oil before setting out for a party is one such precaution. If you can't face it neat, have a small portion of salad with a liberal dose of oil on it. A glass of milk is another precaution. And some people swear by a few forkfuls of mashed potato; but it seems likely that any other absorbent kind of food would do just as well. Who, after all, wants to boil a pan of potatoes before setting off for a party?

Don't be deceived by the superficial mildness of such drinks as sherry. On a few glasses of it strong men have been known to keel over – followed, according to many accounts, by the most excruciating hangover they have ever experienced. And don't mix drinks; don't, for example, down martinis followed by table wine followed by brandy or port or liqueurs (especially liqueurs) followed by one for the road – one of anything, however innocuous. Avoid cocktails, unless you know what their components are and are sure you can cope with them. Keep clear, at all costs, of mulls and grogs and cups of dubious legitimacy.

If, notwithstanding all these precautions, you feel you have drunk too much (and there are certain indicators to this, like a room that revolves or undulates, or both, simultaneously, or alternately; or a frame of mind that suggest that everyone is your friend/enemy) then try the water cure. It won't help you at the time the indications show up, but it will, or should, avert the death-is-my-only-friend feeling next day.

The water cure is just this: drink as much of it as you can face before going to bed. Keep a big glass of it handy by your bedside. It will taste drab, especially if it is tap-water. But with a bit of luck you will feel as right as rain on the morning after.

Avoid the hair-of-the-dog-that-bit-you. Avoid bitters and the revolting recipes that people (who would know better, if they didn't drink so much) swear by. If you are a victim just sleep a lot and eat as much as you can. And keep on drinking water.

Wine & Food

There is no shortage of advice on what to drink with what. On the contrary, there is a surplus of it. The most familiar exhortation is that you should drink white wine with white meat or fish, and red with red meat, and this is all right as far as it goes, but it doesn't leave much scope for imagination. Many varieties of wine – red, white and rosé – are sufficiently adaptable to be able to bypass that particular precept.

In fact none of the conventions about pairing wine and food are completely inflexible. On the other hand there is not much point in setting out to kick convention in the teeth for the sake of non-conformity. The man who insists on serving Nuits-Saint-Georges with sole bonne femme, or Muscadet with bombe surprise, is likely to find himself out on a limb. The conventional patterns for wine and food pairing make good sense and provide a workable framework for a successful, civilised meal.

Before looking at general arrangements for bringing wine and food harmoniously together it is worth noting that there are some kinds of food which simply won't strike up any kind of accord with wine; and the result of bringing them to the table with wine can be, at best, unsatisfactory, and at worst downright disagreeable. Examples are hors-d'oeuvre or salads with French dressing or significant quantities of vinegar; pickles and pungent relishes; cream soups; heavily spiced dishes like curry and some kinds of Middle Eastern and Central or South American food; cream cheese and other varieties of cheese, like Camembert, which have a musty flavour; puddings that feature, either centrally or incidentally, chocolate or citrus fruit.

The list is by no means a comprehensive one. In general the flavours that will clash with wine are sharp ones, like lemon or vinegar, and fulsome ones, like chocolate.

Aperitif wines Spirits are not, to my mind, the best of aperitifs. After a couple of Scotches or gins-and-tonic the palate is pretty well anaesthetised, which is all very well if the meal you are sharpening your appetite for is mutton vindaloo, but is likely to be a sad waste if it is a classic European menu with good wine.

The best drinks for sharpening the appetite are dry. Sugar tends to leave your hunger part-satisfied even before the meal has begun, and a brisk walk over the park will be a better appetiser than a string of cream sherries or sticky patent aperitifs. Sweet drinks, moreover, have a habit of masking the palate.

None of this, however, rules out drinks that are half-sweet, or are at once sweet and bitter. Some of the most popular aperitifs are in these categories. They include vermouth, usually sweet if it is Italian, dry if it is French, with Cinzano, Martini and Noilly Prat being the best known brands. A comparative newcomer to the range of vermouth styles is sweet and white, the best known brand being Martini Bianco. This is a good party drink, but is too sweet and aggressively flavoured to make a successful aperitif for my taste. One of the most appealing vermouths is Chambéry, from Savoy, notably dry and delicate.

Sherry is the safest of aperitifs to serve for guests, and the medium-dry amontillado the safest of sherry styles. It is one of those uncommon drinks that, if not exactly right for all tastes, is not desperately wrong for most. Fino is the most severely dry of sherry styles, and marvellously whets the appetite and refreshes the palate. Manzanilla is another good dry variety, with a crisp, salty tang which makes it ideal to serve before a meal that features shellfish. But it is worth remembering that these very dry sherries, though widely regarded as the finest of aperitifs, are not to everyone's taste. Some people find their flavour completely acceptable but their impact on the stomach acidulously disagreeable. So there should always be an amontillado or some other alternative.

No kind of port can be as decisively dry as the driest styles of sherry, but a good white port ought to be respectably dry and can make an attractive aperitif. The drier styles of Madeira, Sercial and Verdelho, are excellent.

The most agreeable of aperitifs I know is dry Champagne, especially before a meal at which meritorious wines are going to be served. And Champagne, by its very presence, can work wonders in bestowing a sense of occasion. It is, of course, expensive; if it is more than the budget will bear there are plenty of well-made sparkling wines at more modest prices; nearly every wine-making country produces them.

Then there are straightforward table wines. Not many people have a penchant for red wine unaccompanied by food, but there are many whites and rosés which make ideal aperitifs. Avoid the very driest, which can drop like a dagger on to the gastric juices and are really for drinking with food; and avoid, too, the sweeter whites, which are appetite despoilers. This leaves a great range of medium wines, among them, for example, modest Rhines and Moselles, Vouvray, medium white Bordeaux, Anjou and Cabernet rosé.

All these aperitif wines ought to be cooled in the refrigerator to enchance their freshness and – in the case of the sweeter kinds, and the less dry varieties of vermouth and patent aperitifs – to break their sweetness.

Soup Good consommé and the meatier kinds of meat soup, like thick oxtail, game or kidney soup, can all accommodate any of the drier kinds of fortified wine. Creamy, buttery soups, especially those based on vegetables, and some fish soups and chowders, are usually better without wine. They have a simplicity and charm that wine can do nothing for.

The fortified wine for consommé should be dry or fairly dry, and for such soups I would recommend sherry. Fino will do well provided the consommé is not assertively flavoured, for example a simple chicken consommé. For the stronger flavours it is no bad plan to choose something more stoutly flavoured: amontillado is probably the wine that will best please most people.

Thicker soups, like kidney or game, need something that will not wilt in the face of their flavour. The two drier versions of Madeira are exactly right for this job. Dry though they may be they have a degree of sweetness (Verdelho in particular) that helps to bring out all of the flavour of a well-made meat soup, while the soup obliges in the same sort of way for the wine. Dry Madeira is probably the best wine there is for soups of this nature.

Two other types of soup are good with wine though usually only if the soup is at the centre of the meal – at, say, a supper party. The first is minestrone, which, with plenty of Parmesan cheese, will match up splendidly with one of the lighter Italian reds like Valpolicella or Bardolino. The other is bouillabaisse, which is more of a soup-lapped main course than a straightforward soup. I would open a bottle of good medium-dry white Bordeaux with such a dish, or else one of those fruity whites that come from the Midi area of France. But a modest Riesling from almost anywhere in the world, provided it is well-flavoured, will do just as well.

Choosing wine to complement soup is altogether optional. There is no need to go to any trouble, and certainly no need to go to any expense, to find a wine that will be at home with soup. Good soup can keep its own end up without wine; and it can benefit enormously from a dose of wine, or sometimes, and especially in the case of lobster soup or bisque de crevettes, for example, of brandy.

Hors-d'oeuvre and egg dishes Again, wine is very much of an optional extra, and for the standard run of hors-d'oeuvre it is almost certainly better to opt out. The bits and pieces on the hors-d'oeuvre tray are likely to have a fairly high proportion of vinegar or some other kind of dressing, and these will be best left wineless. Similarly, eggs and wine have no great accord (though a good cheese omelette, served with good bread, is an exception). Grapefruit, if it is the starter, can have some Kirsch (cherry spirit) poured into it, though there is a divided school of thought over whether this enhances or despoils it. Melon, so long as you eschew the powdered ginger that often comes with it, can have a most amiable relationship with white port. Prawn cocktail, or any sort of fish or shellfish cocktail, usually has a high proportion of vinegar in the dressing, so that wine drunk with such concoctions will taste sour.

Fish Sometimes fish comes as an appetiser, sometimes as the course between the starter and the main course, and sometimes as the main course itself. Wherever it falls it usually calls for a dry or dryish white wine. There are some exceptions to this: fresh or grilled salmon can get along famously with a demure red like young Beaujolais; while light fish dishes can be on the best of terms with whites that have some sweetness about them. Fish dishes with a white sauce are especially responsive to this treatment.

Most kinds of shellfish and smoked fish will be on uneasy terms with anything but the driest of whites. Plain shellfish needs plain wine, like white Burgundy, Muscadet or Pouilly Fumé. Oysters are traditionally matched with Chablis, and they could not find a better partner.

These, however, are not the right wines for shellfish that has been wrapped in sauce, such as lobster à l'américaine or thermidor. Choose, for such dishes, something that has a discernible degree of sweetness to it. Riesling is the grape to go for, and German wines are ideal: Moselle for the milder dishes, hock for those that are more assertive.

For plain grilled or fried fish, unsauced, either a dry or a medium-dry white will serve admirably. The rule-of-thumb assessment is to take a dry with an uncomplicated dish, such as plain grilled trout, and a more generous wine with something that has been prepared in a more lavish way – fried in butter, for example.

Wine can, in fact, get along very well indeed with fish in almost every form. A recipe that calls for tartare sauce, mayonnaise, mustard sauce, or even horseradish relish, will not necessarily quarrel with wine, but in such cases it is best to avoid a costly, well-bred wine, for it will probably be wasted.

Meat dishes There are, in essence, four broad categories of main course wines: light reds, of which Beaujolais and Bardolino are examples; middle to lightweight wines, of which claret, Burgundy and, indeed, most of the world's output of reds are examples; dry whites, of which Graves and Soave are examples; and semi-dry whites, exemplified by most kinds of Rhine and Moselle wines, and by most wines made from the Riesling grape in any part of the world.

Some people, of course, have set preferences and will stick by their preference through thick and thin; thus a claret fancier may dismiss Burgundy as unsubtle, and will drink his claret with all kinds of pungently-flavoured dishes that convention would pair with Burgundy or Rhône, which have a reputation for being sturdy and full-bodied. However, if the claret fancier knows his stuff and chooses his claret with care, he should have no difficulty in finding one with sufficient body to cope with strongly-flavoured food. The idea that *all* claret is necessarily lighter in body than all Burgundy is a mistaken one. Similarly the man whose preference is for white wine can always find one, like a good Burgundy or Rhine wine, that will drink pleasurably with red meat and even with game.

All this goes to underline the fact that no-one need stick by the book in matching up food with wine, and that there is infinite satisfaction to be had in experimenting. Experiments, however, are likely to show happier results if certain broad considerations are kept in mind. Among them are these:

1 Light reds may be swamped by very pronounced food flavours. They are at their best with unassuming flavours: examples are veal, plainly prepared lamb, roast chicken and roast duck.
2 Full-bodied red wines may swamp subtle flavours in food. Their best place is with such robust dishes as roast beef, game, roast goose and most kinds of casseroles made with red meat.
3 Dry white wines are at home not only with fish dishes but with most dishes that can accommodate a light red. One important consideration in choosing between a dry white and a light red is the nature of the trimmings and vegetables that will accompany the dish. If a poultry dish, for example, has well-seasoned stuffing or sauce, or both, then all but the most firm-bodied whites will knuckle under, and a light red will be better. Examples of vegetable flavours which will be happier with a red than a white are turnips, artichokes and red cabbage.
4 Semi-dry white wines are mostly on good terms with anything fairly bland, like chicken dishes served with white sauce and plain boiled rice.
5 Rosé wines, if they are dry, can be substituted for dry whites, and the sweeter varieties for semi-dry whites.

Cheese There are no companions more amiable than wine and cheese. I would, however, stop short at choosing a *special* wine to serve with cheese. If the cheese course goes where it should most sensibly go, after the main course but before the pudding, then one of its purposes is to project savoury food beyond the main course and so provide an opportunity to finish that course's wine before moving on to sweeter things.

It is thus the cheese that needs to accommodate the wine, rather than vice-versa. Those that best complement wine, and red wine in particular, are the mild varieties like Derby, Lancashire, Leicester, Caerphilly, Bel Paese and Edam.

More tangy flavours also have a place. Examples are Cheddar, Cheshire, Derby Sage, Double Gloucester and smoked cheese. Blue cheese and wine are by no means incompatible, but such cheese is likely to overwhelm even the most stout-hearted of reds. It follows, then, that blue cheese should never be the sole cheese on the board.

Not all cheese is on speaking terms with wine. Camembert, Brie, and the various goat-milk cheeses have a mustiness which is decidedly unfriendly towards wine. And in much the same category must go most of those cheeses flavoured with such things as peppercorns, garlic or onions. They are all too pungent to be really agreeable with wine. This does not mean that all these varieties should be banished from the board, just that there should not be a preponderance of them in your selection.

Puddings Sweet wine with sweet food is very much an optional extra, especially at the climax of a meal that has already featured rich dishes and two or more other wines. The commonsense strategy is to serve a pudding wine only when there has been just one other wine during the meal. The bonus here is that by avoiding a spread of expenditure over three or four different wines you can afford to buy two really good wines.

The darkest of sweet flavours – Christmas pudding, sticky fruit tarts – need a darkly sweet fortified wine. Sweet Madeira is among the best value in this group of wines. Malaga is a less costly alternative. Port could have a place, but not good port, and certainly not vintage port, which is too valuable to share a place with food of any kind.

More lightly-flavoured puddings can get along famously with the most famous of rich white table wines: Sauternes, Tokay or sweet Champagne. Plain fresh fruit, notably ripe peaches, has a special accord with well-bred Sauternes. But almost any kind of pudding that is not naturally more at home with fortified wine will be on good terms with any of these three outstanding wines.

Some pudding recipes call for wine, usually fortified wine. Obviously there will be discord if any other variety of sweet wine is served with such dishes. Nothing, for example, should be served with pears in red wine or with brandied fruit.

Sweet Champagne, Tokay and the best kinds of Sauternes are all costly. However, all but Tokay have perfectly acceptable alternatives, though none of the alternatives has more than an echo of the honeyed depth of these great sweet wines. It is that quality, which wine-makers all over the world have tried to capture, that puts a premium price on these famous wines.

Spirits at the table Apart from the altogether admirable role fulfilled by brandy at the end of a meal, food and spirits have singularly little to offer one another. Even brandy seems better served away from the table, in the relaxing comfort of armchairs.

There is a handful of exceptions. Good curry is fine with lager, although the combination can be rather heavy. But a long gin-and-tonic drinks enjoyably with curry and other oriental dishes. The combination tends to be rather soporific, and the best time to try it is at Sunday lunch, when there is the opportunity to sleep it off afterwards.

Genever, vodka and other kinds of white spirits, except white rum, can drink handsomely with various kinds of cold, smoked fish.

Various puddings have liqueurs or brandy among their ingredients. Drinking the same kind of spirit specified in the recipe may seem a good idea, but probably, on balance, it is not. If the pudding needed a larger quantity of liqueur, presumably the recipe would have prescribed it. Liqueurs are, in any case, very sweet and have exceedingly concentrated flavours, so a liqueur with a liqueur-filled pudding is not likely to be much of a gastronomic experience.

In the restaurant Not infrequently I drink the carafe wine when I dine in a restaurant, not because I prefer it to anything else there is on offer, but because I dislike the shuddersome mark-up that restaurateurs (with all too few exceptions) impose on wine.

These days most restaurant carafes are filled from jumbo-sized bottles of big-selling brands. The restaurateur has exercised minimal judgement in making his choice, but the chances on average are that the carafe wine will be, if not exciting, honest, clean, palatable stuff. If it is not, send it back, even if it is the cheapest bottle in the house.

Sending back wine of any kind, but especially a more costly bottle, demands not just judgement but fortitude. There must be something plainly wrong with it. Ideally, you should detect this when you take the sample sip the waiter pours. And you must be ready to persevere when your objection meets opposition, which is where fortitude comes in.

In an average restaurant there is no reason to suspect the condition or authenticity of the wine any more than there should be reason to suspect the food. Just appraise, and it is more than likely that the wine will be sound. In case of doubt, ask the wine waiter, if there is one, or the head waiter if there is not, for his opinion. They should be honest men anxious for the success of your meal.

You can try to send back wine simply because, although it may be in perfectly good condition, you don't like it. The chances of getting away with this are slender, and it is not, after all, very reasonable to expect them to be otherwise. You have chosen the wine, on the basis of the information given in the wine list and confirmed by the label. Unless you suspect it is not what it claims to be, you can either lump it or order a bottle of something else. You can always take the first one home to use as cooking wine.

The information in the list is important. Avoid, or at least approach with caution, anything that is sketchily described. For example Médoc, with or without a vintage date. Why is the restaurant so bashful about its background? Why not name the importer or at least the exporter? Perhaps it isn't Médoc at all, but Mongolian red. Perhaps it *is* Médoc, but it has come from fire-damaged stock and is carrying new labels. Restaurants are not usually coy about worthy wines.

Be wary, too, of exotically named wines at fancy prices. A lot of 'new' wine, from countries or districts of countries that have never traditionally been exporters, goes abroad now. You may, for example, come across a southern French wine that has somewhere in its name the name of an expensive French resort. It can *sound* as though it ought to be expensive; but if it is, forget it. Many such wines can be agreeable, but they have no business being highly-priced.

One other caution. Think twice before ordering a wine that is the second cheapest in its category on the wine list. A lot of people are shy of buying the cheapest wine on the list, or the cheapest wine of any group in the list; but they don't want to move too high up the price scale. So they plump for the second cheapest; and that is where the restaurant, if it has a wine to off-load, will put its 'doubtfuls' – indifferent vintages, wines that may have passed their mature best and are going into decline; offbeat wines that sounded like a good idea to the restaurant manager when the wine salesman called and poured a bottle or two, but turned out to be a bad idea. If your choice happens to be the second cheapest on the list, appraise with particular care.

Wine, spirits and smoking In nearly all circumstances – and I cannot, offhand, think of an exception apart from a tobacco company sales convention – it is a mistake to smoke while other people are still eating and sipping their wine. The Edwardians would break for a smoke about one-third of the way through their many-coursed meals for a Russian cigarette. But the habit has faded away, and between-course smokers these days are just about tolerated. Sometimes they are disliked.

They deserve to be disliked at a meal at which worthy wines are served. There seems to be no reason whatsoever why anyone should spend good money on wine and food that is going to be vilified by tobacco smoke. Smokers *can* appreciate good wine, but not while they are smoking; and while they are smoking they spoil the pleasure of others.

So cigarettes, pipes and cigars are for the prelude and the aftermath to a meal, not with it. Between-course smokers at a proudly-wined meal should be crossed off the invitation list.

And no-one can properly assess wine at a serious wine-tasting if tobacco smoke of any kind is swirling around them. Smoking at such an occasion is in order only when everyone has finished tasting.

There are those who doubt whether smokers can appreciate fine wine at all. But smokers can, and do; even heavy smokers. Among them are not a few people in the wine trade. But neither they, nor any other smoking wine-fancier, will inflict the noxious results of the habit on those who do not smoke.

Party Ideas

Drinks parties are not inexpensive, even if you choose a theme as ostentatiously economical as beer-and-sausages. Handing out drinks to your friends these days is like inviting them to dip their hands into your bank account.

You can, however, plan. A drinks-for-friends strategy, if it is carefully worked out, can keep the costs down near to the figure you envisage. It will also avert the gloomy disaster of running out of liquor before the party's over, or the less gloomy prospect of having substantial surpluses, so that you are left to wallow in Bloody Mary and bitter beer for half a year afterwards.

It is better to err on the brighter side, and it need not break you to do it. Ask the wine merchant, in advance, to take back any unopened bottles (he will insist that their seals be unbroken, so don't uncork too many at the outset of the party). The merchant will cross these returned bottles off his bill. Some merchants make a point of offering this facility; others have to be coaxed into such an arrangement.

The play-safe list of bottles for a party provides something for all the usual tastes. On it are (1) sherry – a medium alone will suffice if the budget is very restricted, but a dry should figure too if possible, (2) gin with all its satellite bottles, (3) whisky, (4) beer and (5) tomato and/or fruit juice.

This selection, although it is not large, has something to tempt everyone; the risk is that there may be a run on one particular kind of drink so that you are obliged, when it starts to run low, to put to the guests the hideous choice of switching from gin to Scotch, or vice-versa.

There is a lot to be said for the single-drink theme – laying in a good stock of one kind of drink and offering no alternatives whatsoever, except, perhaps, for juices. This has the risk that Aunt Hilda is going to turn down your theme drink because she's had heartburn ever since she tried it at Biarritz in 1913. In that event there is always the fruit juice or the household drinks cupboard to fall back on.

The best possible theme is Champagne. It has a kind of exhilarating presence even before you actually drink any that makes it the stuff the party spirit thrives on. Champagne cocktails are an alternative, and they need not, of course, be made from Champagne. Choose a fairly dry white sparkling wine, which will do the trick just as well. The recipe I use calls for one lump of sugar, a dash of Angostura bitters, and a tablespoonful of brandy. All these ingredients go into the glass which is then topped up with the well-chilled sparkler.

Sherry is fine for morning gatherings, but, without any alternatives, it can be rather staid as the centre-piece of an evening party. In much the same price range as sherry, and around the same strength, are all kinds of fortified aperitifs that make for an imaginative party without being gimmicky.

One of them is Pineau des Charentes, which has a delightful flavour of brandy and grapes. Less sweet is Lillet, another wine-and-brandy aperitif. Chambéry vermouth is widely regarded as the best vermouth in France, or anywhere else for that matter. It is light, dry and suave with the agreeable flavour of mountain herbs.

Another alternative is Madeira. Choose one of the drier kinds, like Sercial or Rainwater. They have the unlikely quality of being dry enough for most dry tastes but not too dry for those who prefer a sweeter drink.

The best of the get-together bottles for the budget-conscious are natural table wines. They should be either white or rosé, and well chilled. Avoid those that are bone dry. Much of the appeal of thoroughly dry wines is their capacity to strike up a happy accord with certain kinds of food. Unaccompanied by food they can give the digestive system a rude shock.

Wine for this purpose need not be costly, but it is wiser, unless funds are low, to avoid the very cheapest; cheapness is not a pointer to nastiness, but if a wine is nasty this is going to show up all the more when it is drunk without food.

For those with no limitation on the party budget, the sky's the limit. Amaze your friends by serving de luxe brands of vintage Champagne, like Heidsieck Monopole Diamant Bleu, Taittinger's Blanc de Blancs, or Moët's Dom Perignon. Or try liqueurs on the rocks, provided your guests can stay in bed the morning after. Nearly all liqueurs lend themselves to this treatment, and orange curaçao, anisette and apricot brandy are especially suitable.

Another excellent party idea is to hold a home tasting. Comparative tastings are by far the best way to get to know wines, but formal tastings with a wine merchant as impressario have their drawbacks: keeping your tie out of the line of fire at the spittoon; being obliged to sip when you are dying to drink; dodging the enthusiastic grower fresh from the vineyards who wants your opinion on his wine, for whom 'very nice' or even 'excellent' won't do – he wants to know what your *soul* feels, and 5000 words are barely adequate.

Informal tastings are much more relaxing, especially if you stage one yourself. Bolstered with a buffet, they are a good and inexpensive way of paying off in one stroke all the outstanding hospitality you may never otherwise get round to reciprocating.

There is no need at a tasting that is chiefly social and only part serious to lay on spitting facilities. Spittoons and sawdust boxes are really for tastings at which new wine is being assessed, for swallowing new wine in any quantity tends to be an unhappy experience for the stomach. Provide a few candles for the guests to scrutinise their wine against; no-one seems able to resist doing this when there is a handy candle, so it must have some appeal. There should be something to nibble at between wines. Even though the tasting is not wholly serious, nibbles like pickled onions or cocktail olives are to be avoided. Plain biscuits are the best palate cleansers. Cubes of mild cheese won't do much of a palate-cleansing job but at least they lend variety.

Select about ten wines. Too wide a range is confusing; too small a range makes the occasion just another wine party. The ten should all be different, but they should all have something in common.

Moderately-priced Rieslings are an example. Taste five or six different brands from Germany and Alsace against a handful from Italy, Hungary, Yugoslavia, South Africa and California. Or set up ten inexpensive sparklers to see whether there is a consensus that those made by the Champagne method really do beat hands down those made by mass-production methods. Other wines that can be compared are sherries from Spain against South African, Australian, Cyprus or Californian sherry; low-priced double-litres from Italy; clarets from the same vineyard but made in different years; the offerings of half-a-dozen merchants in the way of plain Médoc and Saint-Emilion.

There are scores of other permutations. Drinking the stuff will, with luck, be pleasurable, and detecting and discussing the differences informative and useful in sharpening your buying skill. There can even be a pay-off, for if you and your guests like one wine sufficiently to lay in your separate stocks of it, there ought to be a discount deal to be done with the merchant who supplied it.

The buffet should round off the tasting, rather than run parallel with it. And the ideal wine to serve with an end-of-tasting buffet is a sparkler.

Another money-saving drinks-for-a-crowd theme is mulled wine. It has to be said that heated alcohol, in all its forms, is badly in need of a public relations facelift. Its image has suffered disastrously at the hands of parsimonious party-givers who tilt the kettle more generously than the bottle. Punches, mulls and possets *are* economical party drinks, but there is nothing duller than an over-diluted one. Even that grand old mull The Bishop can emerge from over-dilution as no more than a defrocked, washed-out curate.

But when they are made well these drinks are first-rate and can give a party a great lift. The ritual of making and serving punch is nearly as exhilarating as the drink itself.

Nearly 400 years ago an English admiral threw a party for 6000 guests and chose a punch as the centre-piece. Among the ingredients were eighty casks of brandy, 25,000 limes, eighty pints of lemon juice, five pounds of nutmeg, 1300 pounds of Lisbon sugar and a cask of Malaga.

It was a punch that packed a punch. It was served by a ship's boy afloat in a small rosewood boat. At frequent intervals the boy, knocked cold by the fumes, had to be fished out and replaced with a fresh one.

All these concocted drinks fall into two main categories: the hearteners and the comforters. The hearteners are those with a lot of spirit or fortified wine as their chief ingredient. The comforters are those based on natural wine, ale or cider.

The list of ancillary ingredients is a formidable one. It includes liqueurs, tea, coffee, milk, eggs, oranges, lemons, spices and even, in one case that may be better left unexplored, calf's foot jelly. It is difficult to find any two recipes that agree in all particulars, and some seem to agree in scarcely any at all.

Neither the hearteners nor the comforters demand costly wines and spirits. When wine is stipulated, it should be the cheapest available. When brandy is stipulated, avoid Cognac and Armagnac and choose instead cheaper varieties such as Italian or Spanish. And when a recipe calls for a small quantity of a particular kind of liqueur, there is no need to invest in a whole bottle; a lot of them are available in miniatures, quarters and halves.

The Bishop The ingredients are 12 cloves, 2 fresh oranges, 2 oz. (50 g.) lump sugar, 1½ bottles of port (but port-like dessert wine will do), grated nutmeg and 1 pint (6 dl.) boiling water. Spike one orange all over with cloves and bake in a moderate oven until brown. Rub the lump sugar on the rind of the other orange and place in a bowl, adding the juice of the orange. Quarter the baked orange and add this, then pour in the well-heated port and the boiling water. When the mix is in the glasses, sprinkle each with grated nutmeg.

Budget Mull Heat 2 bottles of red wine with 12 lumps of sugar, half a lemon, sliced, and 6 cloves. Sprinkle with grated nutmeg when poured.

Dr Johnson This is the same as Budget Mull, but you give it a boost by adding a miniature each of orange curaçao and brandy, then calm the whole thing down with a pint of boiling water.

Brandy Punch Simmer the rind of 2 lemons, 6 tablespoons sugar and a pinch each of cinnamon, nutmeg, mace and cloves in 1 pint (6 dl.) water for 10 minutes. Add 1 bottle of brandy and bring close to boiling point. Strain and pour into a warmed bowl with the juice of 2 lemons.

Hot Buttered Rum Slowly stir 6 tablespoons soft brown sugar into ½ pint (3 dl.) boiling water. Add, slowly, 2 flagons of cider (dry, still cider is best). Let this boil and add 1 bottle of dark rum and a small knob of butter and bring back near to boiling point. When poured into glasses sprinkle with cinnamon.

Sherry Posset Warm 2 pints (generous litre) milk in one pan; in another heat 1 bottle of dry or medium sherry and 1 pint (6 dl.) light ale. Add 1 tablespoon sugar to the sherry-ale pan when it is approaching boiling point, then transfer the contents of this to the milk pan, sitrring carefully. Sprinkle with grated nutmeg when it has been poured.

In all these recipes it is important to avoid letting the alcohol boil. You can, if a punch is being served in a bowl, turn down the lights and ignite the surface of the punch – but put the fire out fast, for it's costly alcohol that is going up in flames. Guard against hot liquid cracking your glassware by standing a metal teaspoon in the glass while pouring. Ideally the glasses should be fairly thick and have handles, but sturdy good-sized tumblers will do perfectly well provided they are part-filled only, so that they can be held by the upper part.

Mulls, punches and possets offer a means of converting into something interesting liquids that might, on their own, be rather humdrum.

Wine cups have less justification for existing. Their function is to act as warm-weather coolers, but this is a job that can be fulfilled just as effectively by wine, with no more dressing-up than an hour in the refrigerator will provide.

There are, however, several wine coolers that do have some merit. Like mulls, their recipes do not demand good quality wines; on the other hand, since any dullness in a wine cup will show up far more clearly than in a mull, the very cheapest wines are to be avoided. Choose something that is middle-of-the-road in price and quality for making cups and wine coolers.

All cups need to be chilled. Do not try to achieve this by adding large quantities of ice, for when the lumps melt the cup will be wishy-washy. Use only as much ice as will sufficiently cool the liquor. Better still, thoroughly chill all the ingredients in the refrigerator first, thus eliminating the need to use ice.

An ample jug is the best container in which to make a cup. Ideally it should be of the tight-lipped variety to prevent fruit or ice-chunks from plunging into the glasses. For very large quantities use a bowl and serve with a spoon.

Like mulls and punches, every cup has permutations. The main point on which the recipes differ is whether or not brandy or a liqueur should be added. This is a matter of choice, just as the addition of sugar is, but as a general rule it is probably better to steer clear of a dosage of spirits if you are drinking the cup at hot, high noon, or if it is to be served as a prelude to a lunch or dinner at which more alcohol will be poured.

Badminton Cup This is the recipe with the most sturdily British name. It needs half a small cucumber, peeled and sliced, the juice of 1 lemon, a pinch of nutmeg, 2 teaspoons castor sugar, 1 bottle of light red wine, such as a modest claret, and 1 bottle of soda water. Pour the wine over the solids and stir until the sugar has dissolved. Then add the soda, lemon juice, and half-a-dozen or so chunks of ice. A half sherry glass of curaçao will give the cup more thrust.

Buck's Fizz This drink is known as *Champagne Orange* in France. It is one of the simplest cups to make, and is certainly among the best. It consists of equal quantities of Champagne and orange juice – preferably fresh, though unsweetened frozen orange concentrate will serve. These ingredients need to be well chilled, otherwise the result will taste rather limp. To avoid losing too much of the Champagne's fizz, make this drink in the glass rather than in a jug.

Claret Cup A de luxe version of claret cup also calls for Champagne, or some other sparkling wine: the run-of-the-mill version uses soda water instead. To each bottle of light red wine add a half-bottle of Champagne, or its equivalent in soda water, a glass of sherry, and sugar according to taste. Garnish with lemon peel.

Kalte Ente This mysteriously-named cup (*Kalte Ente* means 'cold duck') is a German speciality. It is a favourite of German wine-growers, who ought to know their stuff. The basis is either hock or Moselle – two bottles of still to one of sparkling – a small bottle of soda water, and half a lemon, sliced. Sugar can be stirred in, and backbone, if it is needed, can again be provided by orange curaçao – in this case a full sherry glass.

Sangria The southern Spaniards reputedly drink sangria by the gallon. This drink is available ready mixed and bottled, but making it for yourself has the obvious advantage of allowing you to get it exactly as you like it. It needs 1 bottle of light red wine – and why not, for the sake of authenticity, a Spanish one – a small bottle of soda water, 2 level tablespoons sugar, half a lemon, sliced, and one or two oranges, also sliced. Stir in a good pinch of cinnamon just before serving. Some sangria *aficionados* add other fresh fruit, like diced apples, pears, melons or peaches, which certainly make the whole thing look very appetising but which rather tend to get in the way of the drinking.

Kir The French are strong on kir, otherwise known as *vin blanc cassis*. You simply pour chilled dry white wine over a dash of Crème de Cassis, a liqueur made from blackcurrants. There is no need to stir, so it is easier made in the glass. Blackcurrant cordial can be used as a substitute for Crème de Cassis, but the result lacks the deliciously fruity flavour produced by the authentic recipe.

This is a sipping rather than a quaffing drink, but you can convert it into a quaffer by serving it in tall glasses and topping up with soda water. Dry vermouth, notably Chambéry, can be used instead of wine or, more extravagantly, Champagne. But the Champagne version is better made with another liqueur, Crème de Fraises des Bois, produced from wild strawberries.

Beer and cider There are things to be done, too, with beer and cider. A pint of sparkling dry cider, a pint of ginger ale and a sherry glass of brandy and you have Bull's Eye. Ale punch needs a quart of chilled brown ale, a glass each of sherry and brandy, a tablespoon of sugar, a pinch of nutmeg and the juice and peel of one lemon.

Cider Cup This is one of the most agreeable of these economical coolers. Pour into a jug a quart of sweet or medium-sweet cider, one bottle of soda water, a glass of sherry and a half-glass of brandy. Add the juice and peel of half a lemon, a tablespoon of pineapple juice and a pinch of nutmeg. The cup can be garnished with a sprig or two of borage.

France
The Cream of the Crop

Opposite *An antique wine press at the old town of Saint-Emilion*

France is the world's pre-eminent table wine producer. Germany produces superb whites, but has no reds of special merit. Italy has reds of considerable merit but whites to please the serious wine drinker are scarce. Hungary has a single jewel – Tokay – but little else that is outstanding. Other countries have wines of great elegance and style and there is hope that, given time, some of these could approach the finesse of some of the best wines of France. But France has been endowed with a greater share than any other producing countries of the world's best wines, and the instinct that turns wine drinkers in the direction of France has a great deal more substance to it than mere custom or tradition.

The French, it needs to be said, are by no means unaware of their position as possessors of most of the world's prized wines. Prices for the best qualities, and even for some of the not-so-good, soared to dizzy heights throughout most of the 1960s and early 70s. The French trade, to quote one of its members (speaking at a time when decent classed growths had finally moved into the luxury bracket), saw this price surge as no more than just and proper. The world was at last placing a realistic value on quality French wines; and the inference was that up to that time the world had been shamefully cheating the French wine farmer.

More realistic Frenchmen saw the continuing price spiral as a potential threat to fine wines. If drinkers were obliged to turn to cheaper varieties, might they not become accustomed to them and, in the course of time, content with them? Who but a privileged few would be able to afford fine wines? How many have caviar as a daily diet?

Some growers themselves took the initiative to dampen the price spiral. The French market, however, in allowing the spiral to run on unchecked for so long was reacting no differently to the pull of demand on restricted supply from any other commercial sector. Some drinkers had been deprived of their favourite bottles, but there was at least a bonus: good wines that had previously had a limited circulation or had been virtually undiscovered found their way to a wider market to sell at reasonable prices. The gap between the top and the bottom of the wine spectrum in the United Kingdom, for example, was narrowed by a big influx of middle-class wines. There is readily available a greater choice of French wines than ever before.

What made France so successful as a wine-producer? Certainly the considerable variations in soil and climate across the country are key factors. But disciplined vines do not grow unaided, or wine make itself, even in the most perfect of conditions. And wine laws, of which France's are the world's most effective and intelligent, may protect fine wines but do not of themselves create it.

The truth is that the French applied themselves with considerable zeal and no little patience to making wine they could admire and enjoy. There are no short routes to creating fine wines, just as there are no short routes to creating haute cuisine. Both call for devotion and inspiration.

There were also, of course, commercial factors. Good wine fetches a good price, and in a country that values good wine there has always been an incentive to make it. The incentive became greater in the latter part of the eighteenth century when France began to sell significant quantities of wine abroad. Wine today is one of the major French industries, earning a substantial slice of the national income. Round about one Frenchman in every seven owes his livelihood to the wine industry.

The most important modern development in French wine history was the introduction of the Appellation d'Origine Contrôlée (AC) laws. The phylloxera blight had created havoc in France; growers made desperate attempts to recover from economic disaster by planting once-great vineyards with mass-producing vines which made much sour, disagreeable wine; misrepresentation was rampant; elementary wine-faking was common. By the beginning of this century the reputation of French wine was in peril.

Various legislative measures were adopted to prevent fraud and misrepresentation. The early attempts were a qualified success only. It was not until the 1930s that a comprehensive package of effective laws was put into operation.

The objective of the laws today is not only to prevent fraud but to encourage producers to achieve and maintain the highest standards of quality. The laws specify the precise limits of each recognised district, and they do so with such exactitude that in some instances single vineyards have their own appellation. They lay down the variety of grape that is to be used to make an appellation wine. They set ceilings on the quantity of any appellation wine that may be produced per hectare. This last requirement is a thorn in the flesh of growers who over-produce (production, clearly, cannot be precisely controlled) for the surplus may not be sold with the main appellation and therefore cannot fetch the same price.

The same restrictions and limitations are applied to a secondary league of French wines, Vins Délimités de Qualité Supérieure (VDQS). These wines are officially rated as not good enough to merit the full AC status, but are above the quality of daily table wines, *vins ordinaires* or *vins de consommation courante*.

Bordeaux

Much of the Bordeaux winefield has precisely the right grounding for great wines – poor soil. The name Graves, one of the most notable areas of Bordeaux, means gravel, and gravel there is, and clay and sand and pebbles, and the vines thrive. The area comprises the whole of the department of Gironde, with the exception of a ribbon of sand dunes

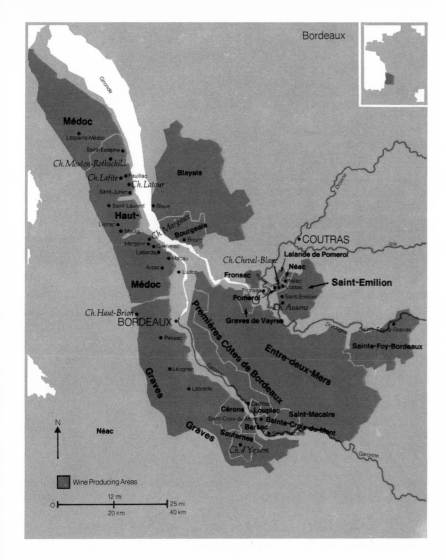

along the coast. Nearly one-eighth of the total land area of Gironde is under vines. Bordeaux produces some ten per cent of all the wines made in France, and about half of the country's fine wines.

Red, white and rosé is produced. The greatest are the reds, known to the world at large as claret, and the superb sweet whites of Sauternes.

Classification of Growths The wines of Bordeaux were divided in 1855 into five leagues, or growths. Only just over five dozen wines were included out of several hundreds in Bordeaux, so the classification was not a comprehensive one. It was confined, in the case of reds, to the Médoc, with one exception, and in the case of whites to Sauternes.

The committee of wine brokers who classified the wines for the Paris Exhibition of 1855 might well be surprised, if they could know of it now, that well over a century later their list remains substantially unaltered. It was probably their intention to draw up an *ad hoc* list. For example, while everything else on their list of reds was from the Médoc, they felt obliged to find a place (in the top class, or *Premiers Crus*) for Château Haut-Brion, which is a Graves. Pomerol and Saint-Emilion were ignored altogether. It was in many respects incomplete, and has been the subject of discussion and argument ever since.

On balance the list has stood up fairly well to the test of time, partly, perhaps, because a place on the list was an incentive to a proprietor to maintain standards. But some of the properties in the lower classifications have shown themselves to be capable of producing, as consistently as is possible in wine-making, quality wines which should

The eighteenth-century Château Loudenne in
the northern Médoc, headquarters of Gilbey S.A.

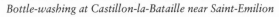

Bottle-washing at Castillon-la-Bataille near Saint-Emilion

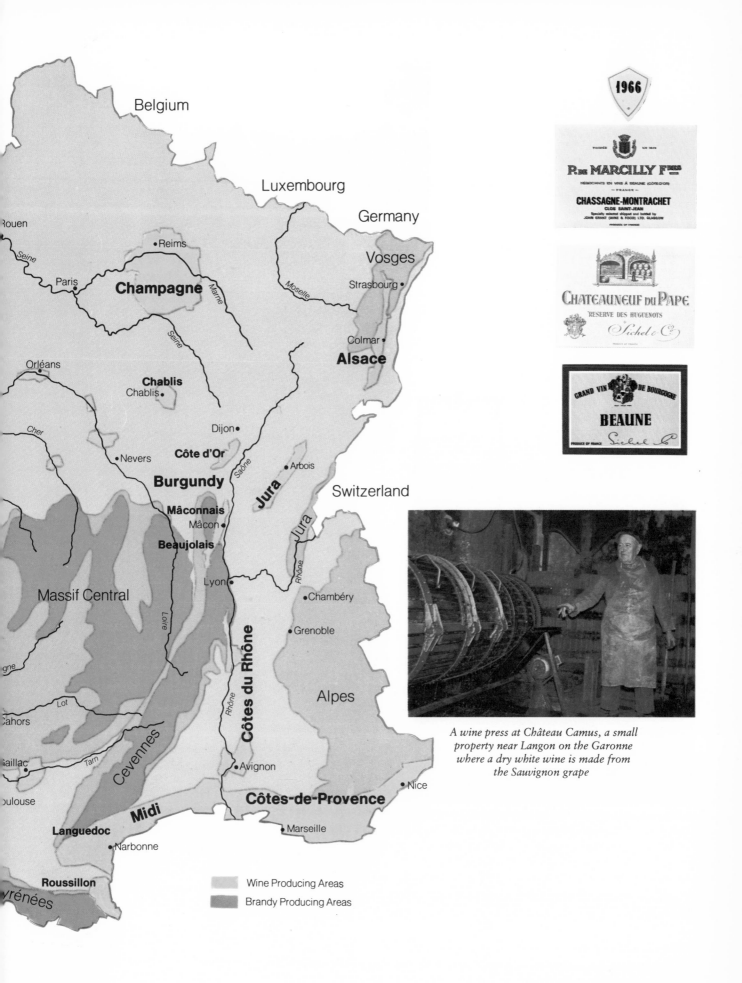

Belgium

Luxembourg

Germany

Rouen

Seine

•Reims

Paris•

Champagne

Marne

Seine

Orléans

Cher

Chablis
Chablis•

Dijon•

•Nevers

Côte d'Or

Burgundy

Saône

Massif Central

Loire

•gne

Lot

Cahors

Gaillac

Tarn

oulouse

Narbonne

rénées

Moselle

Vosges

Strasbourg•

Colmar•

Alsace

•Arbois

Jura

Jura

Rhône

Switzerland

Mâconnais
Mâcon•

Beaujolais

Lyon•

Côtes du Rhône

Rhône

Cevennes

•Avignon

Midi

Languedoc

Marseille•

Switzerland

•Chambéry

•Grenoble

Alpes

Côtes-de-Provence

•Nice

Roussillon

☐ Wine Producing Areas

■ Brandy Producing Areas

1966

FONDÉE DE 1845

R. DE MARCILLY FRES

NÉGOCIANTS EN VINS À BEAUNE (CÔTE D'OR)

— FRANCE —

CHASSAGNE-MONTRACHET

CLOS SAINT-JEAN

Specially selected shipped and bottled by
JOHN GRANT (WINE & FOOD) LTD. GLASGOW

PRODUCE OF FRANCE

CHATEAUNEUF DU PAPE

RÉSERVE DES HUGUENOTS

Sichel & C°

PRODUCE OF FRANCE

GRAND VIN DE BOURGOGNE

BEAUNE

Sichel C°

PRODUCE OF FRANCE

*A wine press at Château Camus, a small
property near Langon on the Garonne
where a dry white wine is made from
the Sauvignon grape*

entitle them to promotion. Some unclassified wines have shown themselves to be worthy of classification. Some classified wines have not done well for some years, and could be candidates for relegation or even for de-classification.

However, despite regular pressure for a revision of the classification, no major updating has ever been officially undertaken, although in 1973 Château Mouton-Rothschild, which had been rated among the second growths *(Deuxièmes Crus)* was upgraded to the first growth. There, with general agreement that it should have been there all along, it joined Châteaux Lafite, Latour, Margaux and Haut-Brion.

Two things are important to bear in mind over the classification. The first is that wines outside the topmost category are in no sense inferior wines; a second growth is not *second-rate*, nor a third growth third-rate, and so on. All five classes are collectively known as the *Grands Crus Classés* – the top five dozen. The second consideration to bear in mind is that no property, whether classified or unclassified, has a monopoly on making good, bad or indifferent wine. Many unclassified properties make superb wines. So the classification, and all the other classifications of France, whether official, semi-official or unofficial, are no more than a guide on which to form a judgement.

Below the classed growths come the *Crus Bourgeois*, some of them wines of considerable quality, the majority simply good or plain wines at reasonable prices.

RED BORDEAUX (CLARET)

The Médoc Outside France, the village, or commune, names of the Médoc are probably better known than the name of the area itself: Pauillac, Saint-Estèphe, Saint-Julien and Margaux are the most famous of them. The wines from all these small areas have their own distinctive characteristics, as, of course, do the wines from different properties within these areas. The wines of the northerly communes like Saint-Estèphe and Pauillac are built bigger and have more colour than, for example, those of Saint-Julien and Margaux, which are famous for their delicate style.

The broad characteristics of the wines from these important communes are:

Pauillac Handsomely big wines with a superb bouquet. The best-known châteaux are Lafite, Latour, and Mouton-Rothschild.

Saint-Estèphe Full, fruity wines, more forthright than those from Pauillac. Châteaux Cos-d'Estournel, Calon-Ségur and Montrose are the most familiar names.

Saint-Julien Wines of finesse, notable for their lovely fragrance. The three Léovilles – Lascases, Poyferré and Barton – are in this area, and another renowned château is Ducru-Beaucaillou.

Margaux Lighter wines, exquisitely suave and elegant and with a fine bouquet. The area takes its name from the most famous of its châteaux. Other familiar names are Rausan-Ségla and Lascombes.

These four areas lie in the Haut-Médoc, the southern part of the Médoc district. The northern part produces wines of lesser fame, but many of excellent quality.

Graves The name, for the British market, still suggests white wine of not very exceptional quality. The fact is that a considerable number of reds are made, accounting for perhaps one-third of the area's total production, and there are some distinguished wines among them, not least Château Haut-Brion, the red which strayed into the 1855 Médoc classification. Other worthy red Graves are made at Châteaux La Mission-Haut-Brion, Pape-Clément, Haut-Bailly, and Smith-Haut-Lafitte. Red Graves from such properties is well-bred and distinguished, though usually lighter in body than a Médoc. Though they can be inclined to mature early, they have good staying power.

Saint-Emilion and Pomerol Both these districts make claret of a somewhat different character from those produced in the Médoc. Pomerols are full-bodied, well-rounded wines, with an attractive bouquet. The leading property of the district is Château Pétrus. Saint-Emilion's wines are almost rich; they have been called the Burgundies of Bordeaux. The two famous châteaux are Cheval-Blanc and Ausone.

Other areas Plenty of other areas of Bordeaux produce good, sound wines. Fronsac, Bourg and Blaye are examples of districts which have attracted increasing interest in recent years as a result of the escalating price for wines from the more renowned districts. As a rule they are more robust and generous than their better-known kinsmen. Given some time in bottle their flavour becomes less assertive, and these wines present an opportunity to buy, economically, for laying down.

Brands, blends, communes Some of the least expensive clarets are the product of neither a single vineyard nor a single year. Bordeaux rouge, for example, which may or may not be sold under a brand name, will be a blend intended to be representative of an acceptable Bordeaux wine. Those with a district name, like Médoc or Pomerol, will be intended to be representative of the wines of those districts. And those with a commune name, such as Margaux, should, the blender hopes, reflect the characteristics of that commune. Broadly speaking, the more precise the label reference is to origin, the more interesting the wine should be.

WHITE BORDEAUX
There is a tendency to dismiss the whole of the vast production of white wine in the Bordeaux area except Sauternes as rather dull stuff, half-sweet, never wholly dry. This is only partly true. While much of the wine produced is certainly undistinguished by contrast with Sauternes, plenty of good, wholesome wines are made, selling at a price that makes them a feasible proposition for regular drinking. Some can be dry, though never bone-dry; the medium whites make agreeable summer drinking; while the plainer varieties of sweet wines make economical drinking for those with a taste for sweet wine.

Sauternes Indisputably the premier white wine of Bordeaux. The area was classified in 1855; Château d'Yquem headed the list as the first great growth, followed by eleven first growths and twelve second growths.

The best of the wines are golden and lusciously honeyed. The grapes are left on the vines until the last possible moment. As they are shrivelled by the sun they are attacked by a form of mildew, *la pourriture*

Right Must being pumped from a vat at Château Guibeau near Saint-Emilion

Below Harvesting at Château Matras near Saint-Emilion

Centre Aerial view of the Garonne valley near Langon

Far right The steep streets of the old town of Saint-Emilion, which is set on an escarpment amidst the vineyards of the Dordogne valley

noble – the noble rot. It takes off some of the water, and the dehydration concentrates the sugar in the grapes. In the most renowned châteaux the grapes are gathered on a selective basis daily, taking only those that have reached a satisfactory state of rot in the previous twenty-four hours. This is a costly process carried out only at châteaux which have the kind of reputation that will make the effort and the cost rewarding.

The famous names of Sauternes, in addition to d'Yquem, include Guiraud, La Tour-Blanche, Lafaurie-Peyraguey, Coutet, Climens, and Rieussec.

Much Sauternes is sold simply as Sauternes, or under a brand name. Too much should not be expected of it; the rich, luscious sweetness of a well-bred Sauternes is never inexpensive.

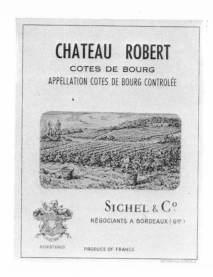

Cérons This area lies between Sauternes and Graves. It makes sweet wines which are never as sweet as Sauternes. Some dry wine is also made.

Sainte-Croix-du-Mont A commune of Entre-deux-Mers which makes pleasingly sweet wines. They do not have the depth of flavour of a good-class Sauternes, but possess something of its distinction.

Loupiac Produces wines that are not significantly different from those of Sainte-Croix-du-Mont.

Graves The best of the white wines are dry. Some producers of red wine make white also, Château Haut-Brion being a notable example. Another dual-product property, Château Olivier, also makes an excellent dry white. No kind of dry Graves has the clean, exhilarating finish of a good white Burgundy, but then few wines have, and Graves at least has the merit of being modestly-priced.

Entre-deux-Mers This area was known once in the United Kingdom for its rather unexciting sweet wines, bought by those who could not, or did not want, to pay the price of even a plain Sauternes. Now the wines from this area must be either dry or medium-dry. They have no special distinction, but are agreeable enough.

Graves de Vayres This district has its own appellation. The white wines here are among those that are a cut above the average white Bordeaux, being somewhat more generous in body and having a suave finish.

Burgundy

All over the world Burgundy is known as a full red wine – just any kind of full red wine, irrespective of its origin. The name has been freely borrowed by winemakers everywhere to identify heavier reds, distinguishing them from lighter reds, which they may call claret. Some years ago the *New Yorker* carried a cartoon showing a wine waiter offering a bottle of Burgundy to a customer. The caption read: 'Oh, French; do they make Burgundy too?'

Genuine Burgundy comes from a long stretch of winefields running from Dijon in the north to Lyon in the south. It produces a variety of styles, not all of which are by any means full, fat reds. Some of the finest wines, notably those from the Côte de Beaune, are white. Some

A Burgundy cellarman sampling wine in his tastevin at Mâcon in southern Burgundy

*Harvesters at Château Matras near
Saint-Emilion*

47

of the better reds are comparatively light, subtle wines.

Choosing dependable Burgundies has always been a problem for wine merchants and customers. The vineyards were mostly in the hands of the church at the time of the French Revolution. They were promptly seized by the State and subsequently carved up and sold to small-time wine farmers. This pattern of small, sometimes uneconomic, parcels of land survives today. The famous vineyard of Clos de Vougeot, which extends to only fifty hectares, is split up among more than fifty proprietors.

This may sound all very egalitarian, but it creates problems. Not all the proprietors have the same ideas about wine-making. Not all are as efficient as the most efficient. The result is that one vineyard can, in a single year, produce *different* wines, all entitled to bear the name of that vineyard.

RED BURGUNDY

Burgundy is a relatively northerly wine area, so that in some years there may be insufficient sun to give the grapes as much sugar as they must have if they are to yield wine with a respectable alcohol level, which is what holds a wine together and gives it its keeping power. There is a solution to this: a treatment known as *chaptalisation* (after its inventor, Dr Chaptal) in which sugar is added at the fermentation stage. Not all Burgundy is given this treatment, and it is said that it does not happen at all to the best qualities. Nevertheless it is a practice that is sufficiently widespread, and sometimes sufficiently overdone, to have created an impression that Burgundy is a slightly sweet wine. Such wines are not representative of even an averagely decent Burgundy.

There was a time when there were very marked differences between Burgundy and claret. Red wine drinkers were divided into followers of one or the other. Now the difference is still considerable, but it is less emphatic, for the character of Burgundy has altered, and the claret fancier could just as easily be a Burgundy fancier.

A combination of developments has brought about the change. The use of fertiliser, for example, has created juicier grapes. But the most important development has been a change in the traditional method of vinification. In the old way, the *méthode ancienne,* most of the grapes were pressed along with their stalks, from which the must derived large quantities of tannin.

Now grapes are destalked before pressing, with the result that the wine is less heavy in tannin and, consequently, lighter to the taste when it is ready to drink. And it is ready to drink sooner, for it requires a shorter period in which to mature. This, indeed, was one of the principal objectives in altering the system of vinification, for the grower has a faster and therefore a more economic turnover.

What all this means is that Burgundy, for the most part, is no longer the great, massive wine that tradition says it should be. It has not become thin or austere; its main characteristics are still fullness, fruitiness and warmth. But it is not the solid wine that past generations knew.

The traditional wine is not completely a thing of the past. Some makers continue to use the méthode ancienne, and some wine merchants make a point of buying stocks for those whose preference is for wine of the old style.

One important difference between Burgundy and Bordeaux is that, while in Bordeaux only communes have an appellation, single vineyards in Burgundy have an appellation of their own in addition to the commune appellation. This situation underlines the individuality of

Top *Grapes being brought from the fields to the co-operative winery at Parnac near Cahors. This is a very large co-operative which handles most of the produce of the many tiny but expanding vineyards of the Cahors district*

Centre *Bottling at Puisseguin co-operative near Saint-Emilion*

Below *Barrel-loads of grapes arriving at Puisseguin co-operative*

the Burgundians and their wines. The communes have a multiplicity of vineyards entitled to give their wine the commune appellation, but the famous vineyards within the commune will use their own appellation. Some names, however, link the name of the more important vineyards in a commune to the name of that commune's most famous vineyard. In Gevrey-Chambertin, the village of Gevrey linked the name of the famous vineyard to its own name; while the vineyard of Mazis is allowed to call itself Mazis-Chambertin.

The Côte d'Or The heartland of Burgundy, with the majority of the renowned vineyards. It is divided naturally into two parts by a break in the mountains, the northern part being the Côte de Nuits, the southern part the Côte de Beaune.

Famous commune names in the Côte de Nuits are Fixin, Gevrey-Chambertin, Morey-Saint-Denis (where the Clos de Tart lies), Chambolle-Musigny, Vougeot (with its renowned Clos de Vougeot), Vosne-Romanée (the home of several outstanding reds, Romanée-Conti and La Tâche being examples) and, perhaps the best-known commune of all, Nuits-Saint-Georges.

The wines of the Côte de Beaune are in general rather lighter in body than those of the Côte de Nuits, and are likely to mature sooner. The main red wine communes are Aloxe-Corton, Pommard, Volnay, Santenay, and Beaune itself, which is the home of the Hospices de

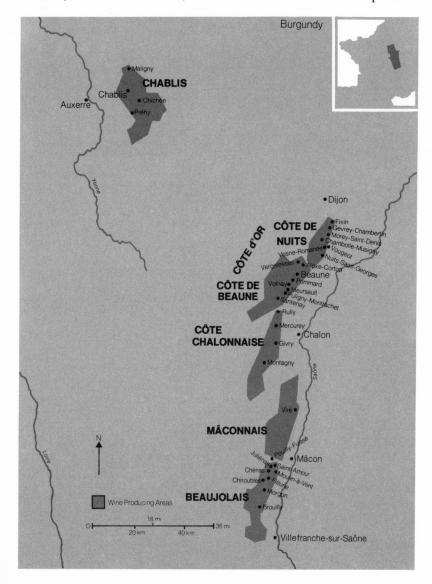

Beaune, maintained by an annual sale of wines. The sale, one of the most important events in Burgundy, attracts buyers from all over the world.

The Côte Chalonnaise Here are made fairly light wines not unlike those of Beaune. Notable communes are Givry, Mercurey and Rully.

The Mâconnais This extensive area produces both red and white wines, the whites being the better. The red wine is fairly light, and therefore not slow to mature. It also has the merit of being relatively inexpensive.

Beaujolais The red wines of this area are uncharacteristic of Burgundy. They are lightweight and fruity and are made to drink young. Much is sold simply as Beaujolais, which is a blend of the better wines from various communes. The best are the commune wines, with engagingly attractive names like Saint-Amour, Fleurie, Chénas, Chiroubles, Moulin-à-Vent and Juliénas.

Beaujolais *vin de l'année* is made for drinking in the spring after it has been harvested. *Vin de primeur* is made and bottled between November 15th and December 15th each year and is intended for immediate consumption.

WHITE BURGUNDY
For grandeur and elegance, the world has no dry white wine which can approach the stature of the best white Burgundies. It has depth of flavour, roundness and a clean finish – attributes that are seldom found in any single white wine. All white Burgundy is dry, which makes it a wine that does not have a large popular following. This, however, has not prevented the prices of the best qualities from moving up sharply in recent years, for they are in demand, and production is not large.

The best kinds can improve in bottle, but most white Burgundy ought to be drunk within a couple of years of the vintage. Qualities vary immensely, but it is useful to remember as a broad rule that the cheaper varieties, while agreeable enough dry wines, are unlikely to show even a hint of the bigness of the best. White Burgundy is one of those wines for which it is well worth paying extra to get the best.

The Côte de Beaune This is the home of the finest white Burgundy. Puligny-Montrachet and Chassagne-Montrachet are among the famous communes. Between them lies the vineyard of Le Montrachet, widely held to be the greatest of all the white Burgundy vineyards. It has only eight hectares, so that production is small, and the wine is rare and expensive. Nearby are outstanding vineyards: Chevalier-Montrachet, Bâtard-Montrachet and Le Cailleret. All have a place among the finest white wines in the world.

There are two other communes of world renown. Aloxe-Corton devotes most of its space to red wines, but the vineyard of Corton-Charlemagne is capable of producing wines that are comparable with those of Montrachet. Meursault concentrates on white wine, which it makes magnificently. Their style is dry, round and almost voluptuous. Great vineyards are Les Perrières, Les Genevrières, Les Charmes and La Goutte d'Or.

Chablis This area produces splendidly dry, almost steely, fresh wine. The terrain is difficult and the ground is hard to work, with the result

Grenache

Syrah

Muscat

Traminer

Cabernet Sauvignon

Sylvaner

Gamay

Sémillon

Cabernet Franc

Riesling

Sauvignon

Pinot Noir

53

that the total production of Chablis has been on the decrease as men leave the district for less arduous and probably better-paid work. Notable vineyard names are Blanchots, Les Clos, Valmur, Grenouilles, Vaudésir, Les Preuses and Bougros, all classed as great growths, and Chapelot and Fourchaume, two of the twenty-two first growths.

The Côte Chalonnaise Agreeable wines, but having less strength of character than whites from the Côte de Beaune or Chablis. The best known communes are Mercurey, Montagny and Givry.

The Mâconnais This area produces large quantities of fairly light, and usually inexpensive, dry whites. The most notable name in the area is Pouilly-Fuissé, a wine which has achieved considerable success in the United States. It is a fuller wine than most white Mâcon, less flinty than Chablis, and with a slightly earthy flavour. As a consequence of the rising price of Pouilly-Fuissé, the neighbouring village of Viré has been able to find new outlets for its own wine, usually sold as Mâcon-Viré. It is cheaper and often of comparable quality.

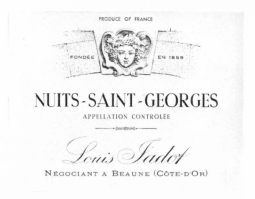

Alsace

Alsace is a white-wine area, and one that is, for France, singularly uncomplicated. The wines, when they are not sold under brand names, are sold under the name of the grape variety that has been used to make them. Sylvaner, Riesling, Gewürztraminer, Muscat and Pinot are the best known outside Alsace. Other varieties are used to make plain wines. A blend of plain wines and one or more of the noble grape varieties is known as Zwicker. One which is blended solely from wines made from the noble varieties is known as Edelzwicker.

Other names are not vastly important. It is usual for a producer to add the name of the town in which his business or home is located. Riquewihr and Ribeauvillé are examples. The commercial centre is Colmar, birthplace of the sculptor of the Statue of Liberty. Some vineyard names are used, such as Ammerschwihr, Kaysersberg, Obernai and Wolxheim.

Gewürztraminer A pungent, spicy wine. The word *gewürz* means spicy. In a hot year Gewürztraminer can have some sweetness, but usually it is quite dry. A *spätlese* (wine made from late-gathered grapes) will be a little sweet.

Riesling This is, of course, the best-known of all grape varieties. In Alsace it produces a very stylish wine, usually dry and attractively fruity. Some spätlese is made.

Sylvaner A fairly plain dry wine, but an agreeable one. It makes a good inexpensive aperitif wine.

Pinot Blanc and Pinot Gris Pinot Blanc is not unlike Sylvaner, though it can have more style about it. Pinot Gris is usually marketed as Tokay d'Alsace, because it is thought that the grape came originally from the Tokay area of Hungary, but it is in no way like Tokay wine. Tokay d'Alsace has considerable body. It ranges from dry to slightly sweet.

Muscat d'Alsace A good, very dry wine with much fruitiness.

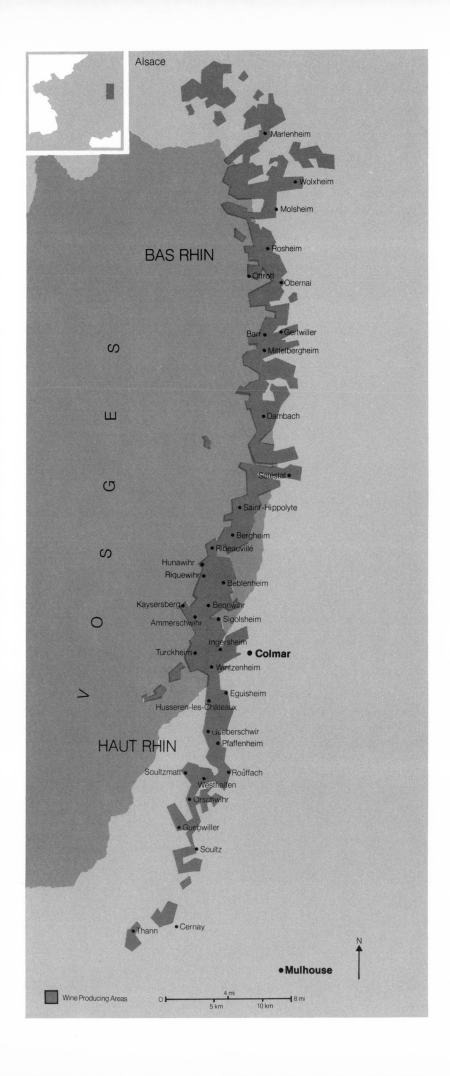

Alsace

BAS RHIN

VOSGES

HAUT RHIN

- Marlenheim
- Wolxheim
- Molsheim
- Rosheim
- Ottrott
- Obernai
- Barr
- Gertwiller
- Mittelbergheim
- Dambach
- Sélestat
- Saint-Hippolyte
- Bergheim
- Ribeauvillé
- Hunawihr
- Riquewihr
- Beblenheim
- Kaysersberg
- Bennwihr
- Ammerschwihr
- Sigolsheim
- Ingersheim
- Turckheim
- **Colmar**
- Wintzenheim
- Eguisheim
- Husseren-les-Châteaux
- Gueberschwir
- Pfaffenheim
- Soultzmatt
- Rouffach
- Westhalten
- Orschwihr
- Guebwiller
- Soultz
- Thann
- Cernay

N

- **Mulhouse**

◼ Wine Producing Areas

0   4 mi   8 mi
5 km   10 km

Top *Kaysersberg, Alsace, one of the most beautiful and typical little towns of the region*

Above *Early morning mist over the vineyards above Kaysersberg*

Right *These timber-frame houses at Kaysersberg are typical of the architecture of Alsace, dating from the sixteenth century onwards*

Left *Harvesting near Santenay, at the southern end of the Côte de Beaune in Burgundy*

Below *Harvest-time vines at Kaysersberg*

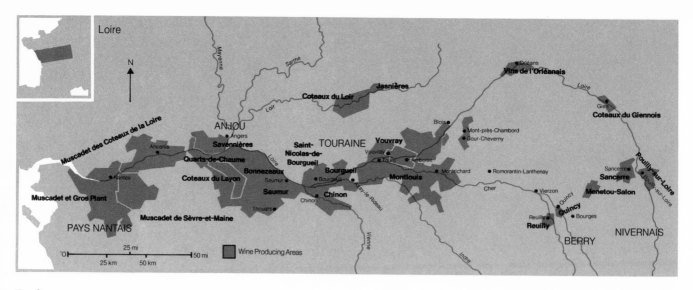

Loire

You could spend half a lifetime sampling the wines of the valley of the river Loire, and the other half giving them a really serious examination. The Loire runs from the Cevennes to the Bay of Biscay, on a course of some 1000 kilometres, and with a profusion of wine varieties more diverse than any other part of France.

There are no great wines in the Loire, but many graceful wines. Wine-growing is very substantially a part-time affair, conducted by farmers who cannot depend for their livelihood solely on wine. Quality, however, is achieved by the co-operatives, which make and market the wines. In addition there are some large private growers.

LOIRE REDS
These are abundant, but worthy qualities are so far scarce. In Touraine, however, two wines have steadily been reaching a wider market: Chinon and Bourgueil. Chinon reds are flowery and soft, with an appealing bouquet. Once or twice in a decade, perhaps, the district will produce handsome wines, with velvet smoothness.

Bourgueil has a special distinction. Here, alone in the Loire valley, only the reds and the rosés may take the district name. Whites must be content to call themselves Touraine whites. The reds are fairly light, with a distinctive bouquet. It is notable that here, unusually in the Loire valley, the soil is rather gravelly and sandy – good wine terrain.

LOIRE WHITES
Loire whites range from the bone-dry wines of Sancerre to the per-fumed, rich sweet wines of Quarts-de-Chaume. Many of the wines offer exceptionally good value for money by today's standards.

Anjou Most famous for its pink wines, but its best whites are rated by many to be the best in the whole of the Loire valley. The sub-district of Savennières is the home of these: the wines are dry, crisp, and yet with good body. Saumur also produces good whites, dry but with a slightly sweet after-taste. In the Coteaux du Layon are the vineyards of Quarts-de-Chaume, producing unusual light sweet wines with a bouquet that is more flowery than a Sauternes.

Muscadet With upward moving prices in Burgundy, Muscadet has proved itself to be an agreeable and modestly-priced alternative. It is

light, dry and fresh. It is a wine to drink extremely young. The best appellation is Muscadet de Sèvre et Maine.

Touraine Here Vouvray is king. It is a silky dry wine, though it can take on some sweetness in a specially good year. In a bad year it can taste astringent. Some of the Vouvrays have an attractive *pétillance*.

Pouilly-sur-Loire This is the home of Pouilly Fumé, a white that takes its name from its characteristic hint of gun-smoke. It is delightfully dry and refreshing.

Sancerre Here are made pleasing crisp whites, tending sometimes to sharpness in a poor year.

Rhône

The 200-kilometre stretch of vineyards known as the Côtes du Rhône, running from Lyon down to Avignon, produces a wide variety of wine. The best-known are reds, but there are some meritorious whites, and the Rhône is also the birthplace of one of the finest of French rosés, Tavel. It is a hot, arid area, making wines that are powerful and heavy in alcohol, although in recent years there have been changes in production methods which have had the effect of making these wines somewhat milder, and faster-maturing, than once they were.

RHONE REDS

Rhône reds have been called 'the poor man's Burgundy', because of their massive character. They are often said to be unsubtle. Certainly they are unlikely to please those who prize refinement and delicacy in wine.

Côte Rôtie The reds of the 'roast slope' are robust and strong. They have a splendidly rich colouring, and there is a trace of flowers in the bouquet.

The 'Cellarmen of Burgundy' who provide light entertainment during the banquets of the Confrérie des Chevaliers du Tastevin at Château Vougeot (Côte de Nuits). The Confrérie is perhaps the most famous wine fraternity in the world

*Robert Dugast with his cellarmaster Georges Tiellit in
his vineyards at Monnières near Nantes on the Loire.
M. Dugast produces 50,000 bottles of Muscadet each
year, of which almost half is for export to Britain*

Right *The château of Saumur was built at the end of the fourteenth century and was further fortified in the sixteenth century. Saumur is famous for its* vins mousseux *and for the renowned cavalry school*

Below *The château and town of Saumur seen across the Loire*

Hermitage From here come more big reds, vigorous and full of body. They can improve remarkably if given only a couple of years in bottle.

Crozes-Hermitage produces hearty reds of a style resembling those of Hermitage, its neighbour, but never as good.

Saint-Joseph Here there are wines for those who may find the sheer weight of many Rhône reds somewhat overwhelming. The reds are lighter in body, and have more poise and subtlety.

Cornas The reds of Cornas show to their best advantage if they are kept for a year or two. Drunk too young they will taste harsh and unfinished.

Châteauneuf-du-Pape This is probably the best-known name among the Côtes du Rhône wines. When Avignon, not Rome, was the seat of the Papacy, this was the location of the papal summer palace – the 'new château'. More than a dozen grape varieties are used to make differing wines, all of which can be given the district name. Their common features, however, are great body, softness, and a pleasing depth of vinosity in flavour.

Gigondas A near neighbour of Châteauneuf-du-Pape, which produces wines with similar characteristics, but usually lacking the same backbone.

RHONE WHITES
Many of the red wine producing areas also make whites, including Châteauneuf-du-Pape, but with two exceptions they are unremarkable.

Château-Grillet This is the most important of the exceptions. It covers only about two hectares and is the smallest appellation contrôlée vineyard. The wine it makes is pale gold in colour, very full, and dry. In a good year it can be superb. But production amounts to between 100 and 200 cases a year, and the wine is scarce and expensive. The surrounding district of Condrieu makes wine of the same style but never with the same breeding.

Hermitage Here the whites are dry, delicate, and have a good bouquet and fruity flavour. The best known name is Chante-Alouette.

Lesser wines of France

The great wine-producing areas are not the beginning and the end of the wine story of France. Of the country's ninety departments no fewer than sixty produce wine on a commercial scale. Many of the wines from outside the great areas were, until a few years ago, oddities outside France, and many, indeed, were oddities outside their own district of origin. Now, with wine merchants scouring France for good quality wines at modest prices, these wines have begun to travel. In the United Kingdom, notably, there has been a considerable surge in wine drinking in recent years, and these low-priced lesser wines have found a ready market.

There are those who write off as necessarily inferior anything that

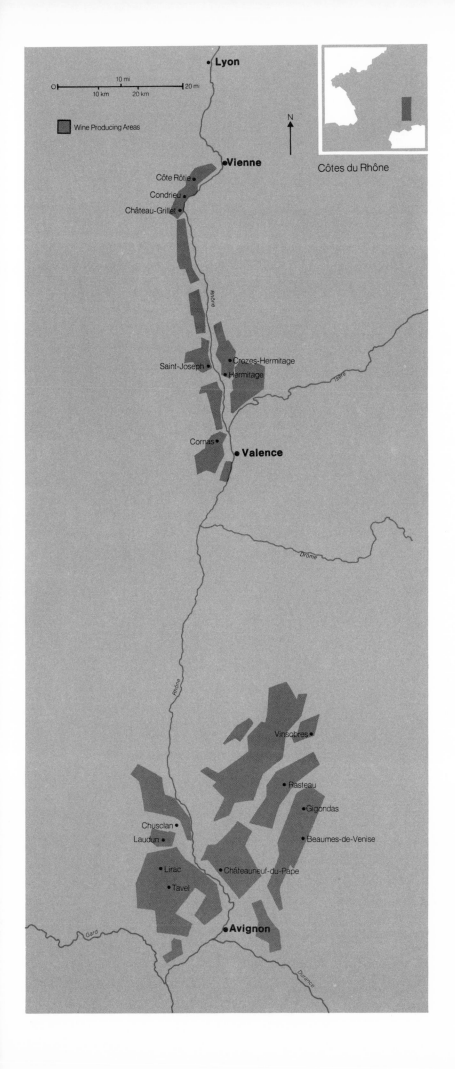

Côtes du Rhône

Lyon

Vienne

Côte Rôtie
Condrieu
Château-Grillet

Rhône

Saint-Joseph
Crozes-Hermitage
Hermitage

Isère

Cornas
Valence

Drôme

Rhône

Vinsobres

Rasteau

Gigondas

Chusclan
Laudun
Beaumes-de-Venise

Lirac
Châteauneuf-du-Pape
Tavel

Gard

Avignon

Durance

Wine Producing Areas

N

0   10 mi   20 mi
  10 km 20 km

comes from outside the classic areas, by which they mean Bordeaux and Burgundy, dismissing the Loire and the Rhône and everywhere else. This is stupid snobbery. It is better to drink agreeable wine at agreeable prices than to drink little wine, or to drink none at all. And many of the lesser wines can equal, or surpass, the lower and sometimes the middle grades from the great areas. A birthplace in Bordeaux or Burgundy is not an automatic guarantee of quality.

LESSER REDS

Cahors This is the name of the main town of the Lot department, in the uppermost reaches of the Lot, a tributary of the Garonne. In the vineyards around the town grapes are grown to produce a red wine so dark in colour it is usually referred to as 'the black wine of Cahors'. It is equally dark in flavour, but at its best this wine can be remarkably smooth.

Jura Most of the production in the area is white and rosé, but around the town of Arbois some agreeable reds are made. The best can be pleasantly soft. Sometimes they have a trace of sweetness.

Languedoc and Roussillon This is the area known as the Midi, a great stretch of territory west of the mouth of the Rhône. Its reputation may never recover from the fact that it is the traditional supplier of vin ordinaire, making vast quantities of unexciting wine. Lately, however, there has been some replanting and attractive red wines, among others, have made their appearance outside France.

Provence Best known for its rosé wines, but reds are made in significant quantities. Pleasant wines come from the district of Bandol, a few miles from Marseille, and others are sold as Côtes de Provence.

LESSER WHITES

Bergerac This area on the river Dordogne is most notable for the sweet white wines of Monbazillac. In a very good year they can have the full sweetness of Sauternes, though they never have its elegance. They are, however, inexpensive.

Jura Known for two curious wines, *vins jaunes*, or yellow wines, and *vins de paille* – 'straw wines'. Vins jaunes are made by sealing the juice of late-harvested grapes in barrels for six or more years. A film of micro-organisms forms on the surface of the wine, not unlike the flor on sherry. When the wine emerges it has acquired a deep yellow colour, and has a fine nutty flavour that is reminiscent of the flavour of dry sherry.

Vin de paille takes its name from the system of laying the grapes on straw mats before they are pressed, with the result that they are partially dried by the sun. This procedure can take several weeks. The wine is also yellow, deeply sweet, and has great staying power. It is expensive.

Gaillac Both dry and sweet white wines are produced in this district south-east of Cahors. They are full, pleasant wines, the sweet having a hint of bitterness in the after-taste.

Languedoc and Roussillon More dry and sweet wines come from this large area. Banyuls and Frontignan are the best-known sweet wines. Both are fortified.

Left Pressing grapes at Monnières near Nantes to make Muscadet

Germany

The Riesling grape is rather insignificant to look at: small, yellowish-green – the kind of grape, if it were to be judged on its appearance, that looks as though it needs nourishment. But in Germany it is king, the source of some of the world's most magnificent white wines. It is grown in abundance in other wine-producing countries, but nowhere does the wine that is made from it achieve the golden finesse that is the hallmark of the great wines of the Rheingau, the Moselle, the Palatinate and elsewhere.

The German vineyards are the most northerly in the world. The terrain is difficult; the climate is stern. Had vine cultivation and wine-making not flourished in these German valleys for some 2000 years, establishing an unsurpassed reputation among the world's fine wines, no-one, surely, would have considered the German wine-producing areas as a promising land for wine production. But some of the best attributes of good white wine are created by the unpromising conditions in which they are grown and made; and if great wine is born of adversity, nowhere is the point better made than in these northerly vineyards.

Yet the German wine growers have no monopoly on bringing delectable liquid out of the Riesling grape. Some of the reputation of German wine has been eroded by indifferent wines – wines that, indeed, suffer hideously by contrast with good, well-made Rieslings from other countries. Much German-made Riesling is the best in the world of its kind; but much has been made for the express purpose of turning a quick penny, trading on the world's opinion of German wines, and the result has been that some miserable wines have gone out into the world flying German colours. The world could be forgiven for revising its opinion of German wines after sampling some of these untypical specimens.

These days things look happier. Germany updated her wine laws with effect from the 1971 vintage; the objectives were to clear up the tangle of names and descriptions surrounding German wine, and at the same time to offer much more adequate protection to the consumer. All laws of this kind take some time to show up their deficiencies, but at least for the time being they are helping to make German wine descriptions more explicit, less subjective, and therefore, with luck, of more value to the wine drinker.

The number of vineyard names, for example, has been drastically pruned. Every hamlet had a bewildering variety of individual vine-growing plots, each of which might command a place on a German wine label. Now only vineyards of at least five hectares are entitled to indentify themselves on the label. In the case of, say, a Burgundian vineyard, this ruling would look altogether unjust and arbitrary. Not so in Germany, where it merely tidies up a situation that had to a great extent got out of hand. No boast about the individuality of a vineyard was too puny to find a place on the pedigree of the wine: 'Grown in the select south-west corner of my vineyard' was a good line. 'On the vines planted by my great-grandfather' was another. These are perhaps extreme examples of the kind of tittle-tattle that would once have had an allowable place among the more general descriptions of a wine, and which was beginning to play a part in making Rhine and Moselle wines too difficult for the average consumer to estimate, and was obscuring their origins, never mind their authenticity, in wild and often worthless boasts.

For the wine drinker the most important provisions of the wine laws are those that divide all German wines into three distinct categories. Table wine *(Tafelwein)* is the plainest of these, and it is likely to be the least expensive. It is simply light, refreshing wine, without any specially demanding qualifications. To get into this class, however, it must measure up to certain minimum standards covering, among other things, the variety of grape used in the making and a minimum alcoholic strength. It can come from pretty well anywhere in Germany, so long as the vineyards of its origin have official approval.

Several notches up the scale are quality wines from defined regions. The full title for them is *Qualitätswein*, which may be shortened on the label to show, simply, Qw. Wines that come into this category are subjected to official tasting; nothing that is untypical of the region in which they are made, and nothing that has been badly made, or made from the grapes of a bad harvest, will get this rating. Qw wines will be honest, dependable, middle-priced bottles. Deinhard Green Label is an example of a good, straightforward wine that typifies this category.

Then there is the upper echelon – *Qualitätswein mit Prädikat*. The *mit Prädikat* is important, and the wines in this category are themselves a good deal more important than the Qualitätswein. The category is, happily, shortened to QmP. Candidates for it are also subject to official testing, but there are many other more stringent regulations and conditions which they must meet if they are to qualify. They cannot, for example, be enriched by the addition of sugar, which is of itself a rather heavy demand of any German wine. It means that they can be produced on an appreciable scale only in good years, or in an average year, only in a comparatively small number of specially favoured vineyards (almost certainly those that are south-facing). They must come exclusively from a single area within their defined region and they must be made from a specified grape strain.

There is a list of additional distinctions which QmP wines can attain. *Kabinett* denotes the most straightforward of the quality wines. *Spätlese* is wine made from late-gathered grapes. *Auslese* is a projection of spätlese: only the ripest grapes are used, the less mature being rejected. *Beerenauslese* means that the grapes used were specially chosen for their over-ripeness. *Trockenbeerenauslese* is made from grapes that have been left so long on the vine that *Edelfäule*, the phenomenon known in the vineyards of Sauternes as *pourriture noble* (noble rot), has set in. The grapes are allowed to shrivel on the

Schloss Vollrads at Winkel, in the Rheingau, seen across the vineyards. In this ancient home of the Counts of Greiffenclau are produced some of Germany's finest wines

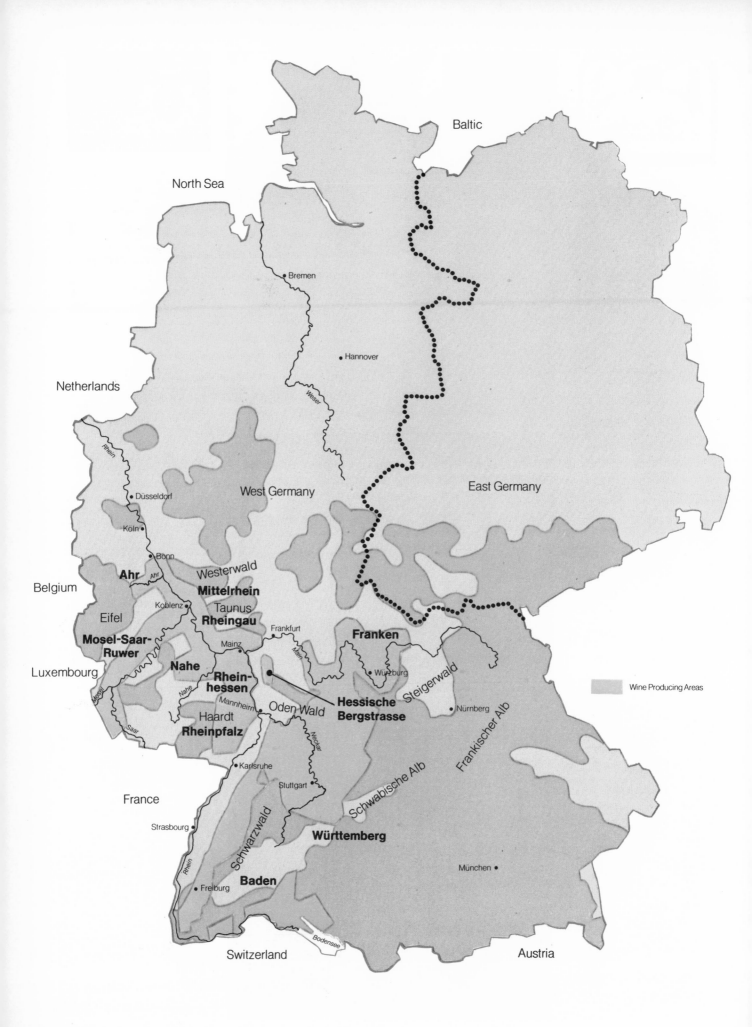

Baltic

North Sea

Netherlands

Bremen

Hannover

Weser

West Germany

East Germany

Düsseldorf

Köln

Bonn

Belgium

Ahr

Ahr

Westerwald

Mittelrhein

Eifel

Koblenz

Taunus

Rheingau

Frankfurt

Franken

Luxembourg

Mosel-Saar-Ruwer

Mainz

Main

Würzburg

Steigerwald

Nürnberg

Frankischer Alb

Wine Producing Areas

Nahe

Rhein-hessen

Mosel

Nahe

Mannheim

Hessische Bergstrasse

Oden Wald

Saar

Haardt

Rheinpfalz

Neckar

Schwabische Alb

France

Karlsruhe

Stuttgart

Strasbourg

Schwarzwald

Württemberg

Rhein

Baden

München

Freiburg

Bodensee

Switzerland

Austria

Top *Riesling grapes at Hochheim on the Main, the origin of our word 'hock'*

Left *Riesling grapes with Edelfäule (*Botrytis cinerea *or 'noble rot')*

Below *Diseased grapes in October, not to be confused with those with* Edelfäule

Left *Harvesters at Nackenheim, south of Mainz in
Rheinhessen*

Above *A cheerful girl harvester in front of Schloss Vollrads at Winkel in the Rheingau*

Left *The twelfth-century church of Kloster Eberbach at Hattenhein, Rheingau*

Opposite page
Top and below right *At Geisenheim in the Rheingau
is one of the most renowned wine schools and
research institutes in the world. Here and below
right a new stem is joined to an old root stock using
a grafting machine which makes an omega cut*
Below left *Müller-Thurgau grapes being harvested
at Winkel, Rheingau*

Below *Antique wine presses in the museum at
Kloster Eberbach, Hattenheim, in the Rheingau*

vine and there is a massive concentration of flavour in them.

One other category is a rarity. This is *Eiswein*, made from grapes that have been left on the vine for so long that they are frozen when they are gathered and pressed. These are superlative wines of honeyed sweetness, but they are few and far between and when they are to be found their price is forbidding.

Each designation, in ascending order from Kabinett up to Eiswein, will be that much sweeter than its predecessor. Auslese in a good year can be rich enough to be a dessert wine, while the categories above Auslese are really wines for drinking on their own. They are much prized by German wine drinkers and their prices reflect this. The best growths of Sauternes are, by contrast, modestly-priced.

One other effect the new laws have had is to edge that old favourite, Liebfraumilch, a few rungs up the social ladder. Once it could be simply any kind of German white wine, and some of it was decidedly ordinary. Now Liebfraumilch must be of Qw status.

There are eleven defined 'regions of production': Ahr, Baden, Franken (Franconia), Hessische Bergstrasse, Mittelrhein, Mosel-Saar-Ruwer, Nahe, Rheingau, Rheinhessen, Rheinpfalz, and Württemberg. Each region has several defined districts, each district a variety of parishes, and each parish a variety of vineyards. Thus a German wine label will these days show the regional name, the district name, the village name and, if the vineyard is sufficiently large to qualify, the vineyard name. Groups of parishes which all make wines of the same general characteristics may use a district name, preceded by the word *Bereich*.

RED WINES

Red wines can be fairly rapidly disposed of. Production of them is not high, and they have no special reputation outside Germany. They may appeal to those whose preference is for lightness in red wine, both in terms of alcohol and flavour. Some, indeed, are so light in colour that they could be mistaken for rosé. The best known kind is Assmannshausen, from the Rhine.

WHITE WINES

Anyone who has ever entered an elementary wine-knowledge competition knows that German wine comes in tall, slender bottles, and that Moselle bottles are green and hock bottles brown. This colour scheme reflects the character of the wines: Moselles are fresh and flowery: hocks fuller and earthier. An important exception to this general arrangement is the *Bocksbeutel* for Franconian Steinwein, a distinctive flask-shaped vessel usually made of green glass.

Grape names are more important in Germany than in most traditional wine-making countries. The newer wine-producing countries are likely to latch on to a grape name as a means of identifying the style of wine you may expect to find inside the bottle; in France, outside Alsace, the grape variety scarcely gets a mention at all, for it is taken for granted that a claret or a Burgundy will be made from the conventional grape of the area. But in Germany the grape variety is likely to get a reasonable display among the smaller print on the label, particularly if the variety happens to be Riesling. This is the grape that makes all the finest German wines – delicate, almost frugal in its modesty, but with an incomparable flavour and bouquet, reminiscent of flowers and fruit.

No other grape variety reared in Germany comes anywhere near this

The little village of Trittenheim in a loop of the Moselle, with the Altärchen vineyards stretching on both sides of the river

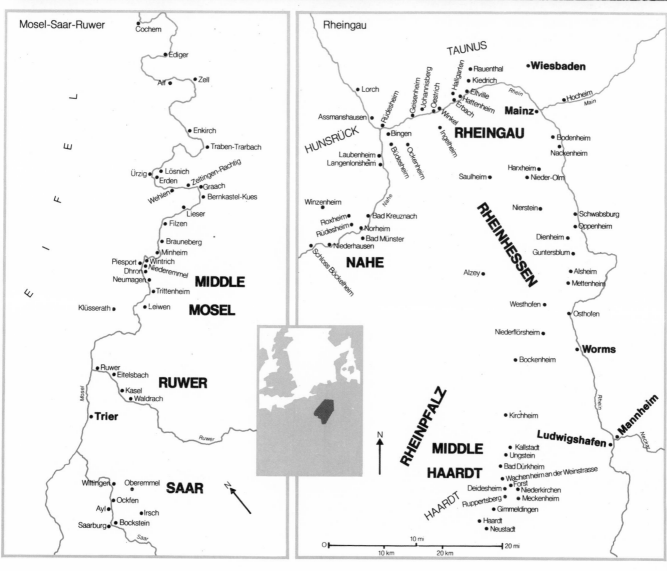

Mosel-Saar-Ruwer

Cochem
Ediger
Alf
Zell
Enkirch
Traben-Trarbach
Ürzig
Lösnich
Zeltingen-Rachtig
Erden
Graach
Wehlen
Bernkastel-Kues
Lieser
Filzen
Brauneberg
Minheim
Piesport
Wintrich
Dhron
Niederemmel
Neumagen
Trittenheim
Klüsserath
Leiwen

MIDDLE

MOSEL

E I F E L

Ruwer
Eitelsbach
Kasel
Waldrach

RUWER

Trier

Mosel

Ruwer

Wiltingen
Oberemmel

SAAR

Ockfen
Ayl
Irsch
Saarburg
Bockstein

Saar

N

Rheingau

TAUNUS

Rauenthal
Wiesbaden
Kiedrich
Lorch
Geisenheim
Hallgarten
Elfville
Johannisberg
Hattenheim
Oestrich
Erbach
Hochheim
Assmanshausen
Rüdesheim
Winkel
Mainz
Rhein
Main
Bingen
Ingelheim
RHEINGAU
Laubenheim
Ockenheim
Büdesheim
Bodenheim
Langenlonsheim
Nackenheim
Winzenheim
Harxheim
Saulheim
Nieder-Olm
Roxheim
Bad Kreuznach
Nierstein
RHEINHESSEN
Rüdesheim
Norheim
Schwabsburg
Bad Münster
Oppenheim
Niederhausen
Dienheim
NAHE
Guntersblum
Schloss Bockelheim
Alzey
Alsheim
Mettenheim
Nahe
Westhofen
Osthofen
Niederflörsheim
Bockenheim
Worms
Rhein
Kirchheim
Ludwigshafen
Mannheim
RHEINPFALZ
Kallstadt
Ungstein
MIDDLE
Bad Dürkheim
HAARDT
Wachenheim an der Weinstrasse
Deidesheim
Forst
Niederkirchen
Ruppertsberg
Meckenheim
Neckar
Gimmeldingen
HAARDT
Haardt
Neustadt

0   10 mi
|----------|----------|
0   10 km   20 km   20 mi

Left *Schloss Ehrenfels on the Rhine silhouetted against the sunset*

Right *Schloss Vollrads near Winkel in the Rheingau amidst its vineyards*

Below *Harvesters on their way to work at Hochheim*

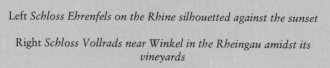

class. Sylvaner (usually, in Germany, spelt Silvaner) is often encountered. It makes gentle, but undistinguished wine. It has been gaining popularity among growers because of its considerable yield – about double that of the Riesling.

Müller-Thurgau is a cross between Riesling and Sylvaner. It makes wine that is less positive than Riesling, but because it yields more grape juice per hectare planted, it is also becoming more common as new stretches of vine-growing terrain are devoted to it. Scheurebe is another cross between Riesling and Sylvaner, and a much more successful one.

Gewürztraminer is the strain that is popular in Alsace. The wine it produces is well-flavoured and almost spicy.

Ruländer is an import from Burgundy, where it is known as Pinot Gris. The wine that is made from it is characterised by a positive, almost assertive, flavour.

Elbling makes scented white wine, most of which is used in the production of sparkling wine, otherwise known as *Sekt*.

Mosel-Saar-Ruwer Wines from this area, known as Moselles in English, are noted for their delicacy and clean finish. The name applies to wines grown not only along the valley of the Moselle river, but to those grown on the banks of its tributaries, the Saar and the Ruwer. Most of the land here is planted with Riesling vines, and the wines are remarkable for their fragrance and freshness. Sometimes they are slightly effervescent, which is natural, and such wines are described as *spritzig*. Two factors combine to make Moselle a particularly suitable wine for drinking with the fish course: it is somewhat more acid than Rhine wine, so that it is able to make a better showing against the fresh flavour of fish, and it is light not only in body but in alcohol, which makes it a first-rate choice at the start of a meal that is going to feature one or more other wines.

The best-rated of Moselle wines are made in the Middle-Moselle; they are bigger-bodied and shorter on acidity than the general run of Moselles. Notable districts in the region are Wehlen, Zeltingen, Bernkastel, Brauneberg, Erden, Ürzig, Graach and Piesport. Notable districts along the Ruwer tributary are Eitelsbach and Kasel, and along the Saar, Ockfen and Wiltingen.

But the most celebrated vineyard in the whole of the Moselle valley is the Bernkasteler Doktor – and that name, needless to say, originates in one of the folklore stories that abound in the world of wine. Some six centuries ago a visiting archbishop was struck down with fever in the town of Bernkastel. All that could be brought to pull him together was a glass of the local wine. After a couple of glasses or so the archbishop fell asleep; but when he awoke on the following day the fever had passed. The churchman attributed his remarkable recovery to the wine, which he described as 'this excellent doctor'. Never slow to follow up a good public relations lead, the Bernkastelers adopted the name 'Bernkasteler Doktor' for their wine – and it has stuck. The vineyard extends to only about five hectares.

The Rheingau Rhine wines have been known in England and other English-speaking countries for centuries as 'hock', and of all the theories put forward to identify the origin of this name, the most plausible is that it is a corruption of Hochheim, a town in the Rheingau. Today, in the United Kingdom, virtually any German wine, Moselle or Rhine, is likely to be offered if you ask for hock. A more precise designation is

Zell-am-Mosel with its steep terraced vineyards above the river

Top *A wine protector surveys the vineyards above
Nierstein, Rheinhessen, from the Oelberg*

Above *The vineyards above Bernkastel on the
Moselle, the home of the famous Bernkasteler
Doktor*

Left *The Pfalzturm near Kalb on the Middle Rhine,
in the mist of an October dawn*

Top *Bar-signs in the narrow Drosselgasse at Rüdesheim, in the Rheingau*

Above *Harvesters, warmly dressed against the chill of a northern October, working in the Steinberg vineyards, near Hattenheim, Rheingau*

Right *On the left a masher and on the right a modern Wilhelms wine press at Ockenheim, Rheinhessen*

Top *Doris Emmerich, the German wine queen for 1974–5, at Waldböckelheim on the Nahe. The Weinkönigin is elected in October at the Neustadt wine festival from candidates who are highly qualified in wine technology, and her duties include promotion of German wines and lecturing at wine tastings such as the one illustrated on page 67. Fräulein Emmerich comes from a family of Winzele (private growers) and attended the wine school and research institute at Bad Kreuznach*

Above *In Germany wine growing is often a family affair. Here the Schmitt family begin a morning's harvesting at Nierstein, Rheinhessen*

a still older one: Rhenish. But no-one knows it any more.

The Rheingau is the Rhine area that is generally reckoned to make the finest of all Rhine wines. There is an immense variety of wines, ranging from crisp, flowery dry to fulsome, golden sweet. They have a particularly elegant style. Hochheim still flourishes, with one of its better-known wines, Viktoriaberg, named after Queen Victoria, who favoured its engaging lightness. Johannisberg is among the best-known of the Rheingau districts and, within it, the famous Schloss Johannisberg, the wines of which fetch prodigious prices. Other esteemed names in the Rheingau include Hallgarten, Hattenheim, Rauenthal, Rüdesheim and Winkel, which last qualifies mainly because of its most reputed vineyard, Schloss Vollrads, producer of splendid, heady wines.

Rheinhessen This area makes a wide range of wines, from plain inexpensive grades, of which there is a great deal, to good and sometimes distinguished wines, of which there is a decent showing. The better wines are notable for their comparative mildness, being generally lower in acidity than those of the Rheingau. The best wines of Rheinhessen come from Nierstein; mellow, elegant and fruity. Oppenheim is the other great district. The wines it makes have more body about them than Niersteiners, and given the right conditions, plenty of sun and not over-much rain, Oppenheimers can be better.

Rheinpfalz (The Palatinate) This is the source of much good, full-bodied wine, often markedly sweet, for the area is one of the sunniest of German wine-producing areas. There are some especially fine dessert wines. The great vineyards lie in the localities of Forst and Deidesheim. Close to Forst lies a hill of volcanic basalt, which retains the heat of the sun and gives it off to the vines after sundown. The famous vineyard here is Forster Jesuitengarten. Important vineyards in Deidesheim include Grainhübel and Herrgottsacker.

Nahe The wines of the Nahe valley are closely akin to Moselles. The river Nahe itself rises near the Moselle but flows into the Rhine, so the similarity is not unexpected. The wines are clean, fresh and rather steely, and the area is reputed to produce the best dry hocks. Great vineyards are Schloss Böckelheim, Bad Kreuznach and Niederhausen.

Franken (Franconia) This area is famous for Steinwein, or stone wine, green-gold wine which can be severely dry, yet deliciously fruity. The name is used today to describe almost any wine of this general character which comes from Franconia, but the finest come from the vineyard in which it originated, Würzburger Stein, a steep hillside over the town of Würzburg. Notable vineyards are Schalksberg, Stein, Harfe, Standerbuhl, Steinmantel and Zurück.

Baden These wines have traditionally been destined for German consumption, but are now finding a wider market. Several varieties of grape are grown, but the Riesling is comparatively rare. The three best areas are Markgräflerland, with Sylvaners, Ruländers and Traminers; Kaiserstuhl, with the same varieties and also some Riesling; and Ortenau, with Riesling, Traminer and Ruländer as well as Blauer Spätburgunder for the production of reds.

Württemberg This area produces much light, refreshing wine, the best of which are Rieslings and Sylvaners.

A centrifugal separator further purifying must in the State wine cellars at Eltville in the Rheingau

Italy

Opposite *Inside the Palazzo Antinori in Florence, home of the Antinori family since the fourteenth century. The family have been making wine since then and are probably the oldest-established successful merchants in Italy*

There was a time when few people took Italian wines very seriously. Methods of vinification were, to say the least, dubious. Wines bearing prized district names were of questionable authenticity. Consistency of style, let alone quality, was not dependable. With a few important exceptions the wine industry was uncontrolled and often uncontrollable; counterfeit wines were not uncommon and 'wine' based on potatoes or cereals or even less wholesome ingredients was sold more or less openly.

With all these question marks it was not surprising that foreign buyers were wary of taking up Italian wines in a big way. Nor was there a great deal of incentive to take them up, for reliable French wines were still moderately priced and the need to scour Italy or other sources of cheap wine had not yet properly arisen.

The world has a long memory and it may take Italy some while to live down the reputation her wines earned for themselves. Even today there are alarming tales of phony wine (but then so are there in France and other wine-producing countries). To be fair Italy has made immense and commendable efforts to put her wine house in order, and they have met with well-deserved success.

One of the biggest factors in encouraging the outside world to invest its confidence in Italian wines is the Denominazione di Origine Controllata (DOC) law. This is the Italian counterpart of the French appellation contrôlée system, guaranteeing authenticity, governing such factors as the variety of grape to be used and imposing ceilings on total production and minimum levels of alcoholic strength.

The DOC law was enacted in 1963. For over thirty years before this many famed and highly-rated wines were protected by Consortia for the Defence of Typical Wines, established by the growers themselves as a defence against faking and name-borrowing. In the Chianti area the consortium obtained legal backing for the territorial limits of Chianti Classico as long ago as 1932. The official limits for Marsala production were established a year earlier.

Even though they had legal backing, however, the consortia's powers were limited, for being voluntary organisations they lacked the power to standardise regulations among themselves and they could enforce their regulations only upon their own members. The need for central control that would guarantee wine from the vineyard to the

consumer was apparent to all who wanted to give Italian wines in general the respectability that many deserved.

The system is under the authority of the Ministry of Agriculture, while the principal body in charge of the law and its regulations is the National Committee for the Protection of the Denomination of Origin of Wines. This comprises growers, wine producers and dealers, members of professional institutions, State experts and consumers. The committee and the Ministry inspectors have the job of ensuring that standards for growing, production, ageing, bottling, labelling and other matters are upheld.

The law can recognise a wine or refuse it recognition. The most obvious candidate for dismissal was white Chianti, which strictly speaking never really existed anyway. Under the DOC laws white Chianti was shown the door, and not a few red wines that used to sail under the Chianti colours have failed to measure up to the standards the committee requires of authentic Chianti. Such wines are now sold under other names, like Tuscan red or white.

For the consumer the law, in essence, means that a wine bearing the DOC seal is what it purports to be and that it is typical of the best characteristics of the district it comes from. Penalties for misuse of the DOC seal or forging a label are severe; a fine of up to £1 a litre and a jail term. In the worst cases the products of the offender can be confiscated and his premises closed for up to a year.

From the DOC system there will emerge, in the course of time, an upper echelon with a State guarantee of quality as well as authenticity. This prospect has spurred on the growers to make voluntary efforts to improve quality, with the result that much of the industry has been revolutionised. Where mixed farming was once the order, with olive trees growing between the vines and hens scratching beneath them, there are now vines alone. The new respectability of Italian wines is more than the result of an image-building job; it is a reality.

Italy is the world's biggest wine producer and the largest exporter. Her main foreign customers are the EEC countries, Switzerland and the United States. Enterprising work by central and regional governments, consortia and shippers has resulted in a massive increase in sales to the United Kingdom in recent years.

Italian wine-producers have, over the years, evolved their own grape varieties. Wine names may, as in the case of Barbera or Vernaccia, indicate the grape variety used or, as in the case of Chianti or Valpolicella, the name of the district in which the wine is produced. Sometimes the name is a combination of grape and district, as in the case of Barbera d'Asti.

Vintage years are not, in general, of cardinal importance in choosing Italian wines, for few of the areas that produce quality wines are subject to violently adverse weather conditions. It is, however, an oversimplification to argue that vintages do not matter at all. The vine is grown all over Italy, in climates ranging from the severity of the Alpine north to the semi-tropical conditions of a southern summer.

RED WINES

Chianti Chianti remains Italy's most famous wine. Something like a million hectolitres of it are produced every year. Most is made to be drunk young, while it is still fresh. Young Chianti is an exuberant wine; light, quaffable, and fairly heady, to be drunk with dishes like escalope of veal Milanese or with grilled pork chops. It is not a serious, subtle wine, although it can be very good indeed.

Since the Chianti area, covering about 70,000 hectares of Tuscany between Florence and Siena, is the best-known one in all Italy, it is no bad place to take a look at how the DOC laws apply. The set of conditions begins with a lengthy list of permitted communes, sub-divided for the various sub-types of Chianti. After this, it gets down to the real details; dealing with terrain, for example, it stipulates that only hill vineyards with the right orientation and at a maximum height above sea-level of 550 metres can qualify.

Then the soil must be right. It must be mainly of sandy chalky substrata with schist or shale that is sandy/clayey. Vines at valley bottoms or on plains are expressly excluded, as are those in pliocene clay or soil that is heavy in clay – even though this cuts out some vineyards that qualified under the old consortium regulations of 1932.

The conditions tell the producer the levels of alcohol and total acidity his wine must have, and stipulate that it must be brilliant in clarity, ruby tending to garnet red, strongly vinous in odour with a strawberry perfume, well balanced, dry, lightly tannic in taste.

Even the bottles have to conform. They must be consistent with the dignity of a good quality wine. If it's a flask intended for export, it must be a traditional Tuscan flask. Crown corks and twist-open capsule closures are forbidden.

Chianti is an 'invented' wine – a wine which owes its formula to thought and experiment. The benefactor was Barone Bettino Ricasoli, landowner and Prime Minister of Italy. Dissatisfied with the quality of the wine available at his castle in the Tuscan hills, he purposely set out to improve it. Without him Chianti would have remained what it was: one of the multitude of the world's little local wines.

The formula calls for four different grape species, and a second fermentation is caused by the addition of grapes at the end of the first. Local farmers borrowed the Barone's formula and methods, and although there are numerous variations on his original notion, the characteristic wine of Chianti today is fundamentally as the Barone conceived it.

Wines from the historic heartland of the Chianti area are sold as Chianti Classico. Controls on yields, harvesting, vinification and ageing have existed in this zone for more than forty years, and the growers' own mark of authenticity – a black cockerel on the label – has for a long while been recognised as identifying classico as being among the most dependable of the several 'district' wines on the market.

Wines from other districts of the Chianti area are, however, made with as much skill and care as classico, and are in no sense second rate. Districts that produce high quality wines in addition to classico include Colli Aretini, Colli Senesi, Colline Pisane, Colli Fiorentini, Montalbano and Rufina.

The young Chiantis, which often have a slight prickle on the tongue, completely natural in a youthful wine, are likely to come in wickered flasks, although the job of making the straw covering and the problems arising from the transportation of these hard-to-pack containers are likely to spell the end for them.

Chianti that is made to be aged is sold in Bordeaux-style bottles, since these can be readily stored in a cellar. Chianti of this kind is known as *Riserva*, and to qualify for this description under the DOC laws it must be aged for a minimum of three years. The finest of the riservas can be aged for as long as six years before bottling. When it leaves the bottle it is round, fragrant and sturdy – a wine to drink with a roast. Some riservas can continue to improve in bottle for a great

Castello della Sala, built in 1350, is the headquarters of the Antinori family's Orvieto estates in Umbria. Here white wine is made from the Trebbiano grape

PIEMONTE
Gattinara
Vermouth
Barbaresco
Barolo
Barbera
Asti Spumante
Cortese

LOMBARDIA
Chiaretto del Garda
Lugana

TRENTINO-ALTO ADIGE
Terlano
Santa Maddalena

VENEZIA
Valpolicella
Bardolino
Soave

LIGURIA
Cinque Terre

EMILIA-ROMAGNA
Lambrusco
Sangiovese

TOSCANA
Chianti Classico
Colli Aretini
Colli Senesi
Colline Pisane
Colli Fiorentini
Montalbano
Rufina

UMBRIA
Orvieto

MARCHE
Verdicchio

LAZIO
Est! Est!! Est!!!
Frascati

CAMPANIA
Lacrima Christi

SICILIA
Corvo
Marsala

Wine Producing Areas

many years and can show much of the elegance of style of a well-aged Médoc.

Because the name Chianti is chiefly associated with a light, fruity wine it is generally played down on the label in the case of a riserva, the maker giving it an individual name that becomes recognised as the best wine of his house. Examples of such names are Brolio Riserva, Riserva Ducale, and Villa Antinori.

Apart from riservas, there is no special merit to middle or old age in Chianti; after a couple of years or so these wines tend to lose the freshness which is essential to their charm. Rather confusingly there is a category known as *vecchio* (old). But this merely means the wine has been aged for a year.

Barolo Chianti may be Italy's best-known wine, but there are many who would argue that her finest is Barolo. It is made from the Nebbiolo, one of the greatest of Italian grape varieties, and it is in the village of Barolo, in Piedmont, that the Nebbiolo performs best.

Deep, dark-coloured and richly scented, it is a match for game or beefsteak. It has to be over three years old before it is drawn from the cask for bottling, and after that it can go on getting better and better in bottle for years. An old Barolo needs a good airing before it is drunk, with decanting taking place perhaps a couple of hours in advance of serving.

Barbaresco This wine has sometimes been called, perhaps not altogether fairly, the poor relation of Barolo. It is made from the same grape, but the result is more lightweight and the flavour less concentrated. Those who look to Barbaresco as an inexpensive substitute for Barolo will probably be disappointed, but appreciated for its own individual merits it is an altogether agreeable wine. It is for drinking fairly young.

Valpolicella From the province of Venezia, this is a lightish red with a good flowery bouquet. It drinks admirably with moderately-flavoured meat dishes or with pasta. Valpolicella is another wine that is at its best in youth, and like the typical Chiantis its reputation has suffered much as a consequence of being kept too long before drinking so that its verve has diminished.

Bardolino This is a close neighbour of Valpolicella, but rather lighter and possibly more subtle. It is one of those wines that are so gentle in flavour they could be mistaken for a deep rosé. It will show to advantage if slightly cooled.

Barbera This is a grape, not a village name. There is nothing sophisticated about it as there is, for example, about Barolo, but it has immense body and great depth of flavour and makes attractive enough drinking with roasts.

Gattinara Like Barbera, this is a Piedmontese wine. It needs at least three years to come into its own, when it becomes lusty and smooth, even if not very distinguished. The Italians, who have a penchant for finding comparisons for the flavour and bouquet of their own wines with a host of other scents, have been known to say that this wine has violets in its bouquet, against a background of tar. Serve it with something hearty but not special, such as meat stew or steak pie.

Lambrusco Not everyone's wine by a long chalk. It may be dryish or semi-dry, and it is somehow voluptuous, which enables it to get along rather well with pork dishes. It pours into the glass with a great surge of froth, like a sparkling wine, but it is only a semi-sparkler, and the foam dies down leaving it prickly to the tongue – a condition the Italians call *frizzante*. Lambrusco is the name of the grape, and it comes from the Modena district.

WHITE WINES

Italy produces a multitude of wines, among which the reds, by and large, offer better value for money than the whites. Good reds are not in abundant supply in every wine-making country of the world; good whites, being less costly to make and having less expected of them in terms of quality, are a good deal easier to find.

Nevertheless, Italy has more than a handful of worthwhile whites, several of which have highly individual characteristics. None, to my mind, has at best more than an echo of the finesse of the classic whites of France or Germany; but then they cost only a fraction of the price of the wines that have a claim to such distinction.

Soave This is the best known. It has a delicious dry freshness and delicacy that is uncommon among Italian wines, making it ideal as a fish-dish wine (it has a specially happy relationship with cold fresh salmon). Soave is a close cousin of the two light reds, Valpolicella and Bardolino, and with them shares the distinction of being one of the famous wines of the Venezia area. Like them, too, it should be drunk young; once it loses its early freshness it tends to taste thin and rather drab.

Frascati Frascati is made in the Alban hills, close to Rome, and is the wine of the Romans. The version that is on the market outside Italy is dry; not as severely dry as Soave, nor as light in body, so that it is good to drink with unspicy veal or pork dishes. There is another version, which I have not so far seen outside Italy, described as *amabile*, meaning pleasant in the mouth. It is, in fact, slightly sweet.

Orvieto This, too, can be either *secco* (dry) or *amabile*. The amabile version is the more interesting. It is made by allowing the grapes to start to rot after they have been harvested. This happens under cover, so that the grapes do not shrivel in the heat of the sun; the result is that they are not heavily sugared at the time of pressing, and the wine is not stickily sweet. It is, indeed, a mildly sweet wine that can be commended to anyone whose taste is for a *partly* sweet wine but has so far failed to find one. Dry Orvieto is a stylish wine, never bone-dry. Either version will complement fairly bland poultry dishes, and the amabile is especially suitable for chicken-and-rice dishes.

Verdicchio This wine is frequently scorned by wine purists as an overdressed poseur because it is often sold in fancily-shaped bottles decked with fanciful labels – and what wine is it, the wine-worldly ask, that needs such trimmings? But Verdicchio comes from the area around Ancona on the Adriatic coast, and the gaudy bottles may well have an appeal for the tourists on the nearby holiday beaches. The wine itself is quite serious, the best being dry with a pale colour and a delicate bouquet. It is dry enough – even verging on bitterness – to drink with fritto de mare.

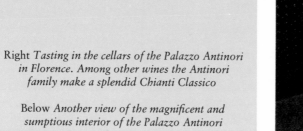

Right *Tasting in the cellars of the Palazzo Antinori in Florence. Among other wines the Antinori family make a splendid Chianti Classico*

Below *Another view of the magnificent and sumptious interior of the Palazzo Antinori*

Left *Glasses of chilled Santa Cristina bianco secco standing on a bar in the Palazzo Antinori*

Below *The mediaeval towers of the Castello della Sala, see page 92*

Est! Est!! Est!!! This is certainly the most easily remembered wine in Italy, if only for the extraordinariness of its name. This derives from the enthusiastic response of the man who discovered it, as it were, for the world. The servant of a German bishop on the way to Rome, he had been sent ahead to sample all the wines he came across en route and to mark 'Est' on the door of any inn where the wine was of good quality.

Est! Est!! Est!!! was the ultimate, found by the servant in Montefiascone, in the province of Lazio. The bishop agreed; he forgot Rome and settled down at Montefiascone to enjoy, so legend says, a life-long binge.

It makes a good story which the wine itself does not completely live up to. It is bright golden, well scented, but not very rewarding to the palate. Like many Italian whites it can be either dry or semi-dry.

Cinque Terre These are dry wines from the rocky vineyards overlooking the Mediterranean in Liguria, which are very well suited to fish dishes. They have an aromatic bouquet and a good rich flavour, yet they are fresh and clean-tasting.

Cortese Rated as the best of all the white wines of Piedmont. It is another fish-dish wine; light, dry and fragrant, but despite its reputation it is not a particularly memorable wine.

Lugana From the district around Lake Garda, this is a dry, fresh and slightly tart wine, with a most appealing opal colour. It tends to be harsh, even sour, in youth, but this is smoothed out after a spell in bottle. It is well suited to the local lake-trout.

Lacrima Christi This is another white that may be more famous for its name than for the pleasure it gives. At its best, this dryish, golden wine, made on the slopes of Mount Vesuvius, is a friendly enough picnic wine. It has a good, summery aroma from one of its constituent grapes, the Greco di Torre. According to the legend, Lucifer, having fallen from heaven, came to earth at what is now the Bay of Naples. He brought with him a small piece of paradise. Looking down one day, God was sad to see the human wickedness that now flourished on this earthly paradise, and shed a tear of pity. It fell on Vesuvius, and on the spot a vine sprang up.

Other wines Golden wines made from sun-dried grapes are a speciality in a number of districts of the Italian wine-producing regions. Vino Santo and Passito are generally sweet dessert wines, but sometimes the juice of the dried grapes is added to dry wine, resulting in a perfumed wine with good body but not overmuch sweetness. Wines of this sort can serve admirably as aperitifs.

Of the multitude of wine styles produced in Italy, the least expected, perhaps, are those of Trentino-Alto Adige in the north. In this alpine region the Alps tower in the north and the Dolomites range eastwards, sheltering the valleys from the north and east winds, while the southerly hills form a barrier against the heat of the plains. All these factors make the area especially suitable for the production of wines of a northern character, and this it does extremely well.

Another important influence is the Austrian legacy, for the Alto Adige was part of the Austrian Tyrol until 1918, and many of the inhabitants remain German-speakers and have a taste for wines of a

style more usually identified with Alsace and Austria. Much of the wine produced in Trentino-Alto Adige is exported to Austria and Germany, but now it is becoming increasingly more readily available in other markets.

Riesling, Traminer and Sylvaner are among the grape varieties cultivated in the area, and it is the wines made from these varieties that are among the most successful. The Rieslings, in particular, hold great promise as stylish, moderately-priced alternatives to German and Alsatian wines for the future. A local speciality is the Terlano grape, which makes a light, greenish-white wine, acceptable enough for summer drinking.

Kiola's vineyards on the steep Langhe Hills in Piedmont, from which comes Barolo, the aristocrat of Italian wines. The Nebbiolo grapes are harvested in late October, and the vintage may even continue into November, when the vines are almost leafless. Vines are trained high here instead of horizontally

Spain & Portugal

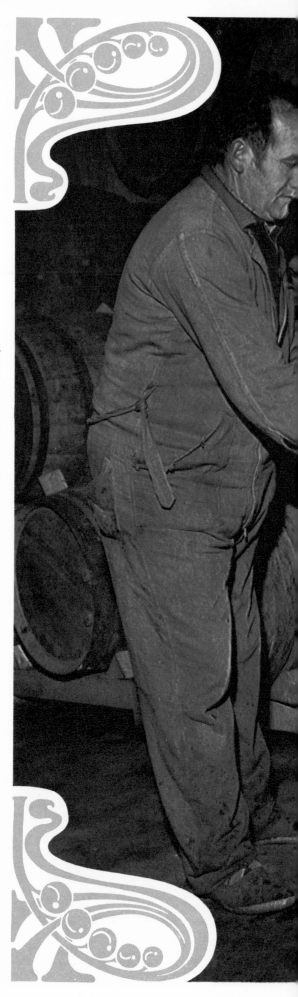

Opposite Taking samples from barrels of red wine
in the Rioja district of Spain

Spain is famous for sherry, Portugal for port, and the table wines of
both, but especially of Spain, have a reputation for being cheap and
unmemorable. Indeed, for many people, the greatest merit of table
wines from the Iberian Peninsula is their modest price; for British wine
drinkers Spanish table wines have for years offered an agreeable and
inexpensive alternative to wines from France and elsewhere. The growing shipments of French vin ordinaire and other plain blends have to
some extent eroded the significant price advantage that Spanish wines
once had, but they remain popular.

Rather oddly, perhaps, Portuguese wines, which are just as cheap
and often better, have never enjoyed popularity on the same scale
abroad, with the mysterious exception of the pink and pétillant Mateus
rosé in the United Kingdom and Lancers in the United States (which
are discussed in chapter twelve). The red and white wines of the Dão
area in northern Portugal are known abroad, but the blends that are
made up for the export market are seldom more than a faint shadow of
the better wines in that area, and tend to be humdrum and unexciting.

This is not to say that the inexpensive, run-of-the-mill Spanish and
Portuguese wines that reach the wider world are mediocre or poor. By
and large they are honest, straightforward wines; but it is one of the
injustices of life that inexpensive wine, like any other cheap commodity, tends to be regarded as second-rate. In fact much wine from
the Iberian Peninsula can beat hands down, in value for money terms,
many French branded wines. A French origin is not necessarily a
virtue.

In the case of Spanish wines the shippers have not helped the image
very much by borrowing French names to describe their product.
All they are trying to do by calling their wine Spanish Chablis, Burgundy, claret, or Sauternes is to give the buyer a hint of what the
broad characteristics of the wine are. No-one even vaguely familiar
with wine is misled by this practice, but it has given rise to a widespread notion that Spanish wines are somehow imitation wines, and
not real wines in their own right. Moreover the descriptions have never
been very accurate. It is true that the heavier reds can sometimes have
some resemblance to the full fruitiness of Burgundy, but the similarity
ends there. And the only common feature of Sauternes and the wines
that are labelled Spanish Sauternes is that both are sweet. A number of

wine merchants have sensibly discontinued the use of these loose and sometimes confusing descriptions.

RED WINES

Both Spain and Portugal have large areas which produce red, white and rosé, but it is the reds which, generally speaking, are most interesting to the outside world, and of those it is the reds of the Rioja district of Spain that have the most serious claim to consideration.

Rioja This area, in the north of the country, takes its name from the Rio Oja, a tributary of the river Ebro. It produces good reds in significant quantity, and much plain wine which finds its way into inexpensive blends on overseas markets, which may well feature the name Rioja in addition to a brand name. But it is important to note that these ordinary wines are not representative of the quality for which Rioja is renowned, and the use of the name on just any bottle is no kind of guarantee that the wine in the bottle will be a cut above any other of the plainer kinds of Spanish wine.

In Rioja they take wine-making rather more seriously than in most other parts of Spain. This approach has its origin in the influence on the area of a number of French vignerons who, when their own vines were hit by the phylloxera bug in the latter part of the last century, crossed the Pyrenees to Rioja, where the vines were still doing well. The Gallic expertise of those days left its mark, and many French techniques are still followed down to the last detail, by contrast with the practice in not a few other Spanish wine areas where wine-making is still a fairly slap-happy business.

One other factor which works in favour of Rioja is the climate. The winters are cold but not harsh; and summers are hot with some rain. This is no bad combination for wine-making.

Rioja reds for export markets are generally well matured. It is the custom in the area to give red wine a lengthy spell in cask; sometimes this can be as much as fifteen years, and the wine is considered to be ready for drinking as soon as it is bottled. These aged wines are known as *reservas*, although a wine that has spent an even longer time maturing will be marked Reserva Especial.

There are light and strong reds, both good, firm fruity wines. They are not comparable in flavour with any wine from elsewhere in the world, but a good reserva is one of the world's most drinkable reds. Producers' names to watch for include Marqués de Riscal, Compañia Vinícola del Norte de España, and Bodegas Franco-Españolas.

Valencia Outside the Rioja area, discussion about Spanish reds begins to flag for want of praise. The reds of Valencia are dark and rich. Sometimes they have an incredibly intense bouquet. More often than not they are rather sweet, and for this reason they are used as one of the component wines in a blend which, when it reaches its export market, will be labelled 'Spanish Burgundy'. Straightforward Valencian wine is scarcely known outside Spain, and inside Spain, while it is acceptable enough, it is unremarkable.

Catalonia Again the reds are heavyweight stuff with no specially commendable feature, and again they are used for concocting blends of one kind or another along with lightweight wines from other areas. The most famous wine of Catalonia is Tarragona, but today wine selling under this mark must be sweet fortified wine – the kind of wine

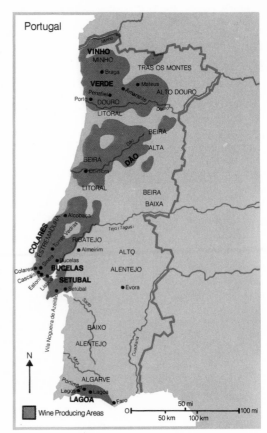

Portugal

Wine Producing Areas

N

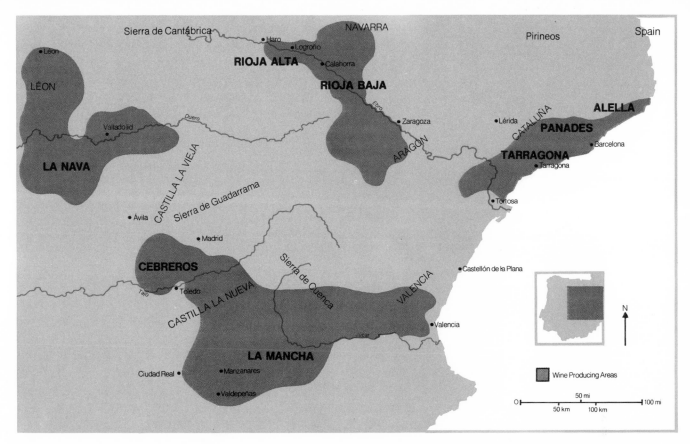

that was once the 'port' in port-and-lemon in English pubs. Tarragona is discussed in chapter thirteen.

La Mancha This is a vast area stretching from Toledo towards Valencia. The reds, for the most part, are undistinguished, but those from the district surrounding the town of Valdepeñas have some interest. Much of the production is on the market in the year following the vintage, although some reds are kept in amphorae to mature for perhaps five years. The young wine is passable enough as a quaffing beverage to accompany a Spanish meal; the matured wine can taste flat and rather dull, the result, no doubt, of having lingered too long before going on to the market. But the name Valdepeñas is worth noting, for it is likely to appear on the label, and should denote an agreeable light red.

Colares Typical Portuguese reds are dark and powerful at the start of their lives, but come round to remarkable finesse when they have been well-matured. The reds produced in the Colares district of the province of Estremadura, where Lisbon is situated, are notable examples of this slow-to-develop characteristic. The best are those that have been left in cask for ten years or more.

Colares itself is an extraordinary winefield. When phylloxera was destroying most of Europe's vines, the vines of Colares survived, for they are planted in sand dunes, and the roots, when phylloxera was moving through the vineyards, were deep and thus to a great extent protected from the plague. Most of the fame of Colares wine was made when it was one of the few wines available.

Colares is no longer a booming wine, but when it can be found (and it should, once found, have several years of age to it) it is rich, warm and satisfying, and as good a red wine as can be obtained anywhere in the world outside the classic regions of France. For commercial reasons

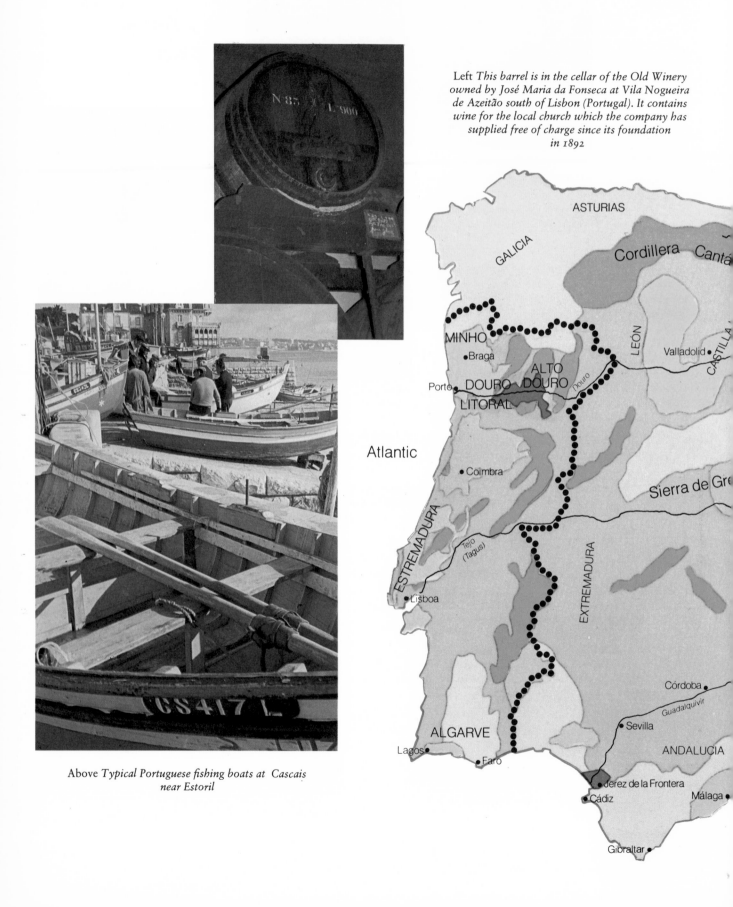

Left This barrel is in the cellar of the Old Winery owned by José Maria da Fonseca at Vila Nogueira de Azeitão south of Lisbon (Portugal). It contains wine for the local church which the company has supplied free of charge since its foundation in 1892

Atlantic

ASTURIAS

GALICIA

Cordillera Cantá

MINHO

Braga

ALTO DOURO

DOURO

LEÓN

Valladolid

CASTILLA

Porto

LITORAL

Douro

Coimbra

Sierra de Gre

ESTREMADURA

Tejo (Tagus)

EXTREMADURA

Lisboa

EXTREMADURA

Córdoba

Guadalquivir

Sevilla

ALGARVE

ANDALUCIA

Lagos

Faro

Jerez de la Frontera

Cádiz

Málaga

Gibraltar

Above Typical Portuguese fishing boats at Cascais near Estoril

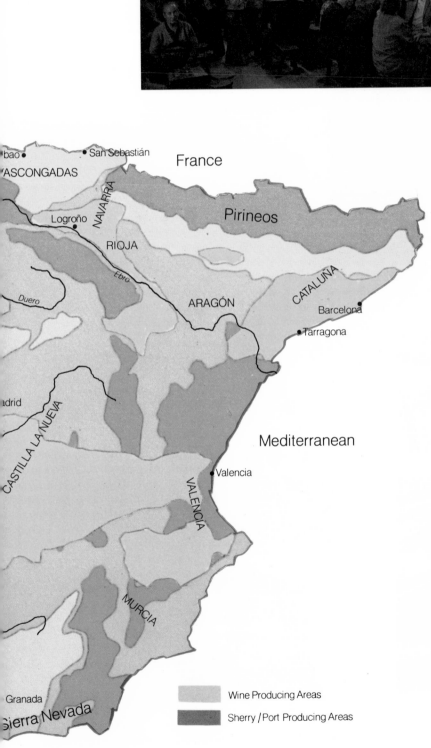

Top *A Spanish bodega at Lloret de Mar on the Costa Brava*

Above *A vineyard worker refreshing himself with local wine in a winter vineyard in the Rioja district of Spain*

France

bao
San Sebastián
ASCONGADAS
NAVARRA
Pirineos
Logroño
RIOJA
Ebro
Duero
CATALUÑA
ARAGÓN
Barcelona
Tarragona
adrid
CASTILLA LA NUEVA
Mediterranean
Valencia
VALENCIA
MURCIA
Granada
Sierra Nevada

Wine Producing Areas

Sherry / Port Producing Areas

the wine-growers have taken to planting vines that yield fast-maturing wines; avoid these. The great grape of the Colares district is the Ramisco.

Dão This pine-wooded, mountainous area in central Portugal has some reds that are modestly handsome, most notably when they are drunk within Portugal. Those destined for the export market seem to be principally designed to sell at a low price (no doubt in competition with Spanish reds) and they suffer in consequence. It remains for some enterprising shipper to lay his hands on a constant supply of sound Dão red.

Minho The north-west of Portugal, between the rivers Minho and Douro, is most famous for its *vinho verde* – green wine, which can be red as well as white. Its main characteristic is the slight prickliness it gives to the tongue, the result of holding carbonic gas within the wine. The reds are fresh and fruity, and agile enough at keeping fever from the brow at an over-warm lunchtime. But like not a few other young light wines, that is the peak of their performance.

WHITE WINES
Both Spain and Portugal have too much sun to be able to produce white wines that are universally acceptable. For most wine-importing countries there are whites just as good and closer to home. It is usually the case that confirmed red wine drinkers are better pleased with what these countries have to offer them than white wine drinkers are with their lot. But this is a generalisation; some Spanish and Portuguese whites are worth attention, even if only for their modest prices.

The white wine route in the Iberian peninsula is substantially the same as the red wine route, for many of the areas produce white as well as red. So we move back to the north of Spain.

Rioja The whites of this area exemplify the considerable quality advantage that red wines have over whites in these two countries. The whites are less markedly agreeable, less obviously an acceptable alternative to pricier whites from other countries. But the growers of Rioja are made of sterner stuff than the growers of most others areas: *their* white is well above average.

The least important of the whites are sold either as Spanish Sauternes or Spanish Chablis. There is no point in dwelling on these. A good, dry Rioja white will be a sturdy wine with some of the austere characteristics of the world's finest dry whites, though it may come across with a slightly earthy after-taste that the drinker of Chablis would not find wholly agreeable. The sweet whites can be generously, though seldom richly, sweet, but they probably represent better value for money than the dry whites. A good brand is Brillante.

Valencia This area produces the kind of wine that is more at home in a wine cup than in a carafe. As a constituent of a blend it does no harm.

Catalonia Here are some well-balanced whites, the most notable of them coming from the Alella area. The vineyards are on mountainsides; those that face north produce wine that is relatively high in acidity, which harmonises very well with the low-acidity wines from the south-facing slopes. Panadés produces a number of dry whites which drink admirably with shellfish.

La Mancha This is the massive wine-factory of Spain. Valdepeñas is the best address for white wines as much as for red. The whites are dry, though the plainest will be somewhat harsh. But the best make pleasing drinking of a light, uninspiring sort.

Montilla-Moriles Strictly speaking the wine of this small area near Córdoba should fall into chapter thirteen, which deals with fortified wines. But Montilla, although it looks like sherry and tastes like sherry, is not usually fortified and does not qualify under Spanish wine law as sherry. The irony is that it was from the name Montilla that the sherry makers of Jerez borrowed the famous sherry name amontillado.

There are dry, medium and sweet Montillas, but it is the dry that has made a name for the wine as a first-rate aperitif. Well chilled, a bone-dry Montilla is one of the best wines for drinking on its own. Most of its merit is in its youth; it is not a wine to buy and set aside for another day, and to be at its prime it should come straight from the cask. Since this is not possible in Britain or the United States, the best compromise is to open the bottle as soon as it has been bought. Never keep the remainder of a bottle to drink even on the following day; it is light, fragile wine and will collapse overnight.

Estremadura This is the home of Portugal's most distinguished red, Colares. But the province also produces a number of palatable white wines. They are not widely shipped abroad, and district names are more likely to be of interest to the traveller in Portugal than to the British or American shopper. Examples are Alcobaça, Almeirim, Torres Vedras, and Bucelas. Bucellas (from Bucelas) had a substantial market in the United Kingdom in the 1900s and was known as a dry, sometimes almost distinguished white. Now it is hardly known at all outside Portugal.

Minho It is hot up here, in the northern part of Portugal, and the grapes are deliberately protected from the sun by the leaves of surrounding plants; they are also trained to grow several feet above the ground, on trellises, so that they are not affected by the reflected heat of the earth, as grapes are elsewhere in the world, or by the small portion of heat that the earth retains after sundown. The vines, and their fruit, are in short defended from warmth, and the resulting wine is as it would be expected to be from sun-starved grapes: light, dry and refreshing.

This is vinho verde – green wine; it is green in the sense that it is young, retaining some of the sparkle of its fermentation, and it is a wine that is intended to be drunk young. Pure vinho verde will be dry but some of the varieties that are sent abroad are sugared a little with the object of making them more acceptable and attractive to foreign tastes.

Dão is probably just about the only wine area of Portugal that anyone outside Portugal has ever heard of, excepting the Douro valley. Things are less green here than in Minho, and drier; farmers are obliged to pump water around their lands in order to ensure that the vines flourish at all. Most of the production is red, but there are several very agreeable whites. They can be dry or fairly sweet, but most of those that find their way to export markets are dry and firm. They are fuller in body than the rather austere vinho verde of the Minho, and offer especially good value among Portuguese whites.

Further Afield

Opposite *Harvesting in the Lutomer Estates vineyards in Yugoslavia*

The whole of the world of wine is dominated, in European eyes at any rate, by France and Germany, and, to a lesser extent, by Italy. But outside these renowned countries there are lands where the vine has been cultivated and wine made for many centuries. It would be unfair to describe them as 'Europe's other winefields', for that description would seem to suggest that all of them are, in some way, second-rate, whereas they are perfectly capable of producing, and do produce, estimable wines. For the most part they are good, honest wines; some of them even have the promise of greatness. But, with one exception – Hungary – there are no fine wines in Europe outside the classic wine countries.

Hungary Hungary's exceptional wine is white and sweet: none other than Tokay. It is the premier wine of Hungary and, as such, needs to be noted first; I will return to it after looking at the good Hungarian reds.

The most famous of the reds is certainly Bull's Blood, otherwise known as Egri Bikavér. It comes from vineyards lying around the old baroque town of Eger, and is made from three grape varieties, the most important of which is a local variety, the Kadarka. Bull's Blood is a big, lusty wine, which has been described as a cross between Burgundy and Rhône; but it is more than that. Over the years it can develop a marvellous smooth silkiness and depth of flavour. It is one of the few comparatively inexpensive wines that is worth laying down.

According to legend, the wine gets its unusual dark red colouring and its body as a result of the addition of ox-blood. No-one need be concerned by this; the colour and the body are both the result of the Kadarka grape, the juice of which is very nearly black.

More wines are made from the Kadarka in other parts of Hungary. They can often show much of the muscle of Bull's Blood. Notable designations are Szekszárdi Kadarka and Vilányi Kadarka. Other worthy reds are made in the area of Sopron, in the north-west of the country.

Tokay is on a par with the great châteaux of Sauternes and the Trockenbeerenauslese of Germany. In its most perfect form it is as luscious as those wines. It is made chiefly from the Furmint grape, which is peculiar to Hungary. The vineyards lie on hillsides in the north-east

of the country, close to the border with Czechoslovakia.

The key to fine Tokay is, as in the case of fine luscious wines else-where, the *pourriture noble* of Sauternes – the noble rot, which leaves the grapes rich and highly concentrated. In Tokay this condition is known as *aszu*.

The ripest grapes are specially selected and set aside in containers, or *puttonyok*. Then all the remaining grapes, whether ripe or over-ripe, are gathered and pressed, but kept separate from the aszu grapes. It is the wine made from these remaining grapes that forms the basis of Tokay aszu; it is, in fact, a blend of two styles of wine. The sweetness of the final product will depend on how many puttonyok of aszu berries are added to the basic wine, and this is shown on the label when the wine is eventually bottled as three, four, or five 'putts'. One that has five will be a very luscious and rich wine indeed, and will be con-siderably more expensive than the others.

But even a five-putt wine is not the pinnacle. There is the fabled Tokay Essenz, which appeared to be in danger of extinction once (as, indeed, were the best wines of Tokay) because the rulers of Hungary since the last World War have been preoccupied with more practical considerations than the production of luxury wine. But about a couple of years ago some bottles of Essenz were shipped to the United King-dom, so it has not been lost to the world.

Essenz is the richest of the juice from the aszu grapes. It is pressed from them simply by the weight of the grapes themselves, while they are lying in the puttonyok. The juice is drawn off before the grapes are pressed and set aside to make this most superlative of all the Tokay varieties.

There is another kind of Tokay, which may be dry or sweet, depen-ding on the state of the grapes at the time of the vintage. This is Tokay Szamorodni, the basic wine, without any added aszu. In an indifferent year most of the grapes used to make this wine will be low in sugar, and the wine will be dry. In a good year the grapes are likely to contain an appreciable proportion of aszu grapes, and the wine will therefore be sweet. Sweet Szamorodni can have a superb bouquet, but will never be as luscious as a Tokay Aszu.

Both Aszu and Szamorodni are sold in elegant skittle-shaped bottles of half-a-litre.

The rest of Hungary has a good showing of sound, agreeable whites, particularly from the vineyards on the shores of Lake Balaton in the south-west. Those with the highest reputation come from the hill of Badacsony. The Kéknyelü grape makes an attractive and aromatic sweet white wine. Other varieties grown around Balaton are Furmint and Riesling. Most of them have more than a hint of sweetness.

A good Hungarian dry white wine is made in the district of Mór, north of Lake Balaton. The grape variety here is Ezerjó, which makes a light-coloured, almost greenish, wine which is good to drink with fish.

Yugoslavia Yugoslavia has a reputation abroad for her good, depen-dable Rieslings, especially those from Lutomer. But some attractive reds are made, among them Prokupac, a fairly light flavoured wine. The Kadarka, the great grape of Hungary's Bull's Blood, is also culti-vated here, though with varying results. Some of the reds can have a touch of sweetness about them.

The Lutomer district is recognised as being the best in all of Yugos-lavia. There are many grape varieties, the most familiar of which

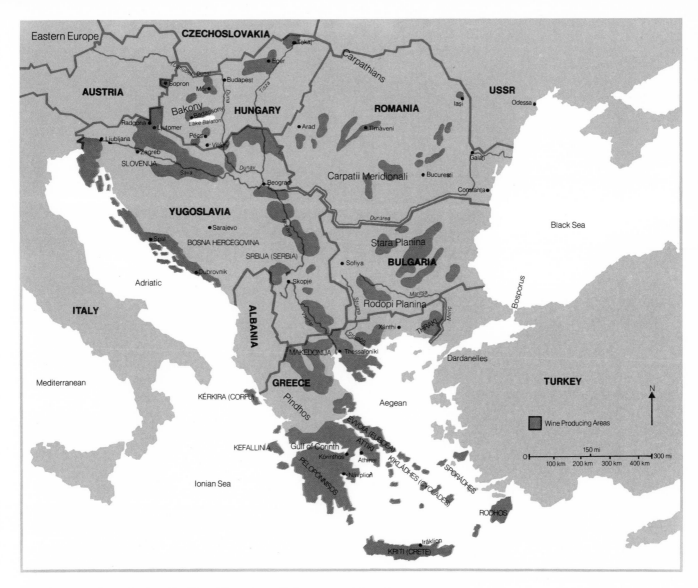

outside Yugoslavia is the Riesling. Traminer, Sylvaner and Sauvignon are also cultivated. As a general rule the grape variety is named on the label, so there is no problem with district names. All the wines have a good, positive flavour. The Rieslings are clean and dry. One familiar branded wine from Lutomer is Tiger Milk, or Ranina Radgona (the names of an estate and a town, respectively). It is made from late-gathered grapes and is sweet, though not lusciously so.

Romania and Bulgaria Both these countries produce significant quantities of wine, their industries having been reorganised since the Second World War mainly with the objective of turning out considerable quantities of plain wine. One of the best of the whites in Romania is Tîrnăve, after the vineyards on the banks of the Tîrnăve river.

The most notable of the reds of Romania are those made from the Kadarka, Pinot Noir and Cabernet Sauvignon grapes, while Bulgaria makes pleasant (and usually modestly-priced) reds from the Melnik and Gamza grapes.

Both countries cultivate a variety of white wine grapes. The Tîrnăve district in Romania has a good reputation, especially for Rieslings, although the most famous wine of the district is a blend of several kinds of grape and is called Perla de Tîrnăve. Bulgaria also uses grapes from other lands, notably Riesling, Traminer and Furmint, as well as a wide range of native varieties.

Left The October vintage at Rust in Austria's Burgenland

Right Locals drink red Kalterer See wine in a Stube in Velden, Austria

Below A harvester with his traditional wooden pannier in the Lutomer Estates vineyards in Yugoslavia

USSR The Soviet Union has, in recent years, considerably expanded her wine industry, a process that was begun in the 1930s when the Government put under way a rapid expansion of viticulture in what were regarded as the finest areas, Armenia, Georgia and the Crimea among them. Production was given a boost when Bessarabia ceased to be part of Romania and was acquired by the Soviet Union.

Most of the wines that are available abroad, both red and white, are Georgian. Mukuzani and Saperavi are reds, the former a flavoursome dry wine, the latter a light one without any very distinctive character. Tsinandali and Ghurdjurni are agreeable whites. Several others are available, but in general the rest of the world has so far had only a glimpse of the fruits of the big development of the Soviet vineyards.

Fragrant light dry white
Blanc de Blanc
Produce of Bulgaria
Shipped and Bottled by Cock Russell Vintners Ltd., London.

Austria This is a country of white wine. Some red is produced but, like Germany's reds, it is of little consequence outside its country of origin.

The leading district is Wachau, in Lower Austria, where the vineyards lie along, and extend from, the banks of the river Danube. Krems is the main town of the area. The simplest wine is made from Austria's own Grüner Veltliner grape; it is light, fresh and fairly crisp. The Riesling is also grown, and produces splendidly scented wines.

Gumpoldskirchen is the other Austrian name of note. A number of grape varieties are cultivated, but the finest wines are Rieslings. In certain years the grapes are late-gathered to make auslese and spätlese wines.

Switzerland Switzerland not only produces wines, red, white and rosé, but also has a considerable thirst for wines, and is one of the world's largest importers. The canton of Valais produces Switzerland's best-known red, Dôle. It is a muscular, well-scented red, made with Gamay or Pinot Noir grapes, or a blend of the two. Those made from the Gamay are rated the best. Other good reds are made at Neuchâtel, while at Ticino, the southernmost canton of Switzerland, some strong, fruity reds are made from the Merlot grape of Bordeaux.

The canton of Vaud is the largest producer of Swiss wines. The vineyards extend along the sunny shores of Lake Geneva to the east and west of Lausanne. The most widely-cultivated grape is the Fendant grape, which is known in France as the Chasselas. Dézaley, Saint-Saphorin, Rivaz and Riex are among important vineyard names. The chief characteristic of the wines is their smooth dryness.

Much white wine is also made in Valais, using, more often than not,

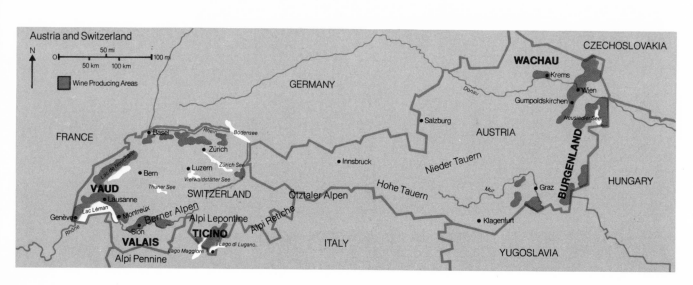

the Fendant. But the Sylvaner is used to make Johannisberg, and Riesling is also made. The white wines of Neuchâtel are characterised by lightness and by a slight effervescence.

Luxembourg This is exclusively a white wine producer. The vines are planted along the banks of the Moselle river. Various vines are grown but one of the most pleasing wines is made from a mixture of Riesling and Sylvaner, which is light but well scented. Lightness of body is the characteristic of most Luxembourg wines; they are proficient thirst-quenchers.

Greece Greece has been in the wine-producing business longer than a great many other countries, but the wines that Socrates and Pericles enjoyed have somehow got left behind in their ancient world. Red and white wines are made in Attica, the Peloponnese, Crete, Macedonia, Rhodes and elsewhere, but they do not have a large following outside Greece. A dependable and palatable brand is Demestica.

The Greeks have a weakness for drinking wine with resin in it. Most of it is made in Attica; it goes by the name of retsina, and is made by adding about one per cent of pine resin to the must. Even in Greece they are not sure how all this began; it may have been when Athens was infested with cholera, and resin was added to wine as an antiseptic; it may have been a result of storing the wine in pine barrels; it may have been to disguise the formidable flavour wine took on after being kept in goatskins. Whatever the reason, the Greeks are devoted to it.

The most frequently exported Greek wines are dessert wines, Mavrodaphne, which is red, and Samos, which is white. Both have a good perfume and make inexpensive wines to drink with sweet dishes.

Cyprus Like other vineyards elsewhere, the vineyards of Cyprus languished under Turkish rule. It was not until the island came into the possession of the United Kingdom in 1878 that wine production started to get on its feet again.

In the past twenty years there has been a considerable expansion of the industry, and much progress has been made in producing wines of greater style. The reds, for the most part, are the most successful. They are made mainly from a local grape variety, the Mavron. The reds have more than a passing similarity to those of southern Burgundy, and are attractively inexpensive. A good brand is Othello.

Cyprus, like other countries in the Mediterranean, has too much sun to be wholly successful with her whites. Some of them have a slightly burnt flavour which can be attractive enough in dessert wines but not in dinner wines. They tend, too, to be rather short, or lacking in after-taste. But they make refreshing, cheap everyday drinking.

Commandaria is the great dessert wine of Cyprus. It is a big, solid, richly sweet wine, made from a mixture of red and white grapes, the red being by far the largest proportion. The finest of it is made in mountain villages, and stored for years in huge earthenware jars. Such wines reach such a high degree of concentration that they need to be blended with other, lighter wines before going on the market.

Commandaria takes its name from the area round Kolossi Castle, built by the Knights of Saint John and the Knights Templar in 1191, who called it 'La Grande Commanderie'. But its history goes back to before that time, and it is probably among the oldest of the world's wines.

Newer Wine Worlds

Opposite *Wines ageing in oak cooperage in a modern Californian winery*

Wherever man has gone wine has gone with him and so, not infrequently, has the vine itself. Wherever it could be cultivated it was planted, and the wine boundaries of the world began to push out of Europe to Africa, North and South America and Australia. For a long while much of the production of these new winelands was fairly basic wine. In comparatively recent years there has been a significant advance in standards and qualities, and not a few wines from these regions have not only shown promise, but have fulfilled their promise, of great merit.

South Africa Some countries have such a long tradition of wine-making that it seems impertinent to label them with the word 'new' at all. In the 1660s the Dutch East India Company had a flourishing trading settlement at the Cape of Good Hope, supplying its merchantmen en route for the Indies; and among the supplies was wine already being produced from the fertile soil of South Africa. The first vines had been planted in 1655.

But the real foundations of South Africa's wine industry were laid by Huguenots who left France during the reign of Louis XIV to settle in the Cape. They brought technical knowledge of wine production which put backbone into the industry.

One noteworthy development at this time was the creation of the only South African wine that has achieved fame in Europe: Constantia, a luscious sweet wine, produced at the beautiful farm of Groot Constantia. It became one of the world's most costly and sought-after wines, but poor imitations hit its popularity, and the market declined. Excellent dessert wines are still made in the Cape, however.

Throughout all the wine-producing districts of the Cape there are pronounced differences in soil, permitting the cultivation of a wide range of vines. A profusion of whites and reds, dries and sweets, can come from within the same comparatively small area.

Good light reds are made from Cabernet and Shiraz grapes in the Constantia Valley and those sections of Stellenbosch lying nearest to the coast. Further inland there are many good heavier-bodied reds using the same grapes as well as the Gamay.

Some very attractive dry and semi-dry whites are made in the district of Paarl, Stellenbosch and Tulbagh. The Riesling grape is particularly

successful here, and fresh, flavoursome wine is produced.

Much of the South African wine industry comes under the umbrella of the Ko-operatieve Wijnbouwers Vereniging (KWV), one of the biggest wine co-operatives in the world. It has a semi-official status and operates strict quality control over wine production. Other important producers are the Nederburg Estate, the Twee Jongege-zellen Estate, Stellenbosch Farmers' Winery, Monis Wineries and Bertrams.

South Africa's main interest is in maintaining and developing her export market for sherries, many of which are of excellent quality and value. There is no large comprehensive range of her table wines on export markets, but a reasonable selection is available in the United Kingdom and elsewhere.

Australia The history of wine in Australia is as old as the settlement itself. The first Governor of the colony of New South Wales prudently brought vines with him when he landed at Sydney in 1788, and promptly planted them. He had, alas, chosen a bad spot; it had too much humidity and the soil was over-rich. Undaunted, the Governor planted a three-acre (1·3-hectare) vineyard at Paramatta, twenty-four kilometres inland, and the early results were so promising that he asked London for technical assistance. London sent him two French prisoners-of-war, on the assumption that all Frenchmen know about wine-making. These were two who didn't, and their efforts did not bear much fruit.

These early experiments had shown, however, that Australia was a hospitable land for the vine, and others followed with more vines. In 1822 Gregory Blaxland shipped a quarter pipe of his Paramatta red wine to England, where it was awarded a silver medal by the Royal Society of Arts.

The main wine-growing areas of the country are South Australia, Victoria, New South Wales and Queensland. The centre of the South Australian wine industry is the Barossa Valley. In New South Wales an important area is the Hunter Valley.

A considerable variety of red wine is produced. The Cabernet and the Shiraz are extensively cultivated. Areas producing good reds include the Hunter Valley in New South Wales, Coonawarra and the Barossa Valley in South Australia and Tahbilk in Victoria.

White wines are, by and large, less interesting than reds. But in the Barossa Valley some excellent wines are made from the Riesling grape, the result, no doubt, of the colonisation of the area by Germans.

Much of Australia's wine production has traditionally been devoted to fortified wines, but in recent years there has been an upsurge of interest among Australian consumers in home-produced table wines. One consequence of this is that there has been extensive replanting and reorganisation to produce higher quality table wines. There seems no doubt that in the course of time Australia's reputation as an important wine producer will be considerably enhanced.

The United States Spanish missionaries were the earliest wine-makers in the United States, cultivating vines in the land round their missions in California and making wine for their own use. They imported a European grape which became known as the Mission, a big producer of somewhat humdrum wine. Planting of classic European vines came later, although the Mission continued to be the most widely cultivated vine in California for many years after the missionaries departed.

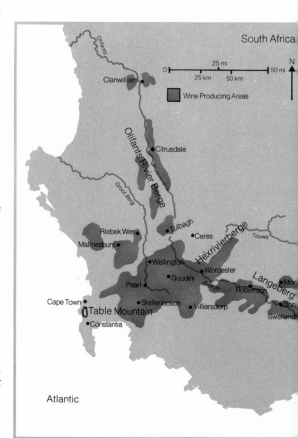

The industry had many birth pains. Speculators and inexpert farmers produced wines of poor quality with dire results for the reputation of Californian wine. Phylloxera struck in the late 1870s with crippling results. Prohibition drove many growers out of the business, for wine was permitted to be made only for medicinal or religious use.

Despite these setbacks, the United States industry not merely managed to stay on its feet, but has expanded massively, with the result that the country has attained a prominent position in the world production league, coming sixth after Italy, France, the Soviet Union, Spain and Argentina. California dominates the US production league with around 300 wineries making more than eighty per cent of all US wine.

In the 1960s and early 1970s the United States experienced a 'wine boom'. The fast-increasing popularity of the drink, particularly among young people, prompted extensive new plantings in California. In 1973 the California Wine Institute reported enthusiastically that newly-planted vineyards, as yet not bearing grapes, totalled more than the whole of the Burgundy apellation contrôlée area. (Comparisons with European statistics are irresistible to Californian wine men.) But in that year there was growing anxiety that the new plantings were going to lead to over-production; and a year later these anxieties became a reality, with many growers being unable to sell their grapes even at drastically reduced prices. Some began to replant with fruit.

Such difficulties, however, are no more than a part of the commercial risks of wine-growing all over the world. California's future as an important wine-producer remains assured.

Since the repeal of the Volstead Act in 1933, there has been steady and impressive progress towards achieving higher qualities. Law, both Federal and State, plays an important part in encouraging this, but still more important is the skill of the Californian industry. Californian producers are recognised as ranking among the world's most advanced

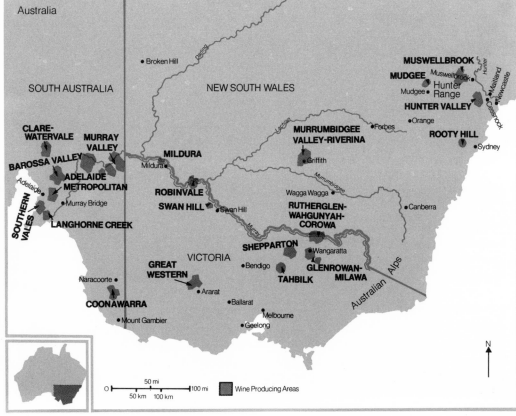

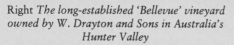

Right *The long-established 'Bellevue' vineyard owned by W. Drayton and Sons in Australia's Hunter Valley*

Below *A heat therapy cabinet at the CSIRO laboratories, Merbein, for heat processing of imported vines to rid them of virus infection. The vines are kept at 37·8°C. (100°F.) for at least 400 days*

121 Opposite page
Left *Vines in the Stellenbosch district of South Africa*

Right *Buckets of Californian wine grapes being dumped into a vineyard gondola*

Below *The gondolas of grapes arriving at a Californian winery*

in vineyard and wine-making technology. The major Gallo winery, for example, was the first in the country to employ research chemists. Wooden fermenting casks have long since been replaced by stainless steel tanks. Blending processes at the winery are computerised. They were (less creditably, no doubt, in the opinion of traditionalists) the pioneers of 'pop' wines – wines that are more like aerated soft drinks, but which nevertheless may have a convincing claim to encouraging young people to take wine in their stride and move on in time to the real thing.

The Christian Brothers, a religious teaching order which began to make wine for sacramental purposes in California in 1882, and to market wine commercially five years later, favour a mixture of traditional and modern methods. Laboratory controls monitor every stage in the production of their wines and brandy, but they take the view that wine-making is the art of a hand craftsman, and as their cellar-master has expressed it: 'Winemakers are babysitters for nature. We set up the optimum conditions, then let nature do her work. We can't push a button or program a computer to transform grapes into fine wines.'

All kinds of wine styles are produced: 'sherry', 'port' and 'tokay' abound, some of them being made at least in part with table or raisin grapes, rather than wine grapes. The best of the wines are table wines made with European grape varieties, and the better producers use the name of the grape to identify the style of wine in the bottle.

The best of the dry table wines are made in the North Coast region, around San Francisco Bay. The Napa Valley in this region is the best of the red wine districts, and the great grape of the district is the Cabernet Sauvignon, making a full, slow-maturing wine. It is somewhat short on bouquet, but otherwise is an excellent wine. Good vineyards include Christian Brothers, Beaulieu, Charles Krug and Louis Martini.

Other red grapes grown in California are the Pinot Noir, the Gamay, the Barbera and several others, less famous. With a few exceptions none of them produce wine as good as that produced by the Cabernet. One extensively cultivated grape is the Zinfandel, which turned up in California around the middle of the last century, though from where, no-one seems to be altogether sure. It makes light, refreshing wine in immense quantities.

The Pinot Chardonnay and the Sauvignon Blanc make some of the worthiest of California's whites. The Pinot Chardonnay performs especially well in the districts of Santa Clara, Napa, Sonoma and Livermore. It is, however, a small producer, and is not extensively grown. The Sauvignon Blanc makes a full-flavoured wine, so much so that its produce is usually blended with that of the Sémillon, which like the Sauvignon Blanc is one of the great white grapes of Bordeaux. The Sauvignon Blanc, the Sémillon and the Muscadelle, another Bordeaux grape, are mixed together to make what is known in California as 'Sauterne' – somehow the final 's' has got lost.

The Riesling, the great grape of Germany which makes very creditable wine in various other parts of the world, does not do so well in California, and the wines it makes are short on balance and general character. The Sylvaner does better, making delicate dry wine for drinking young. There are also Gewürztraminers, with some of the spiciness and aroma of the Alsatian product.

European vines will not flourish in the Eastern states and American natives vines are grown. The main centres are New York, Ohio,

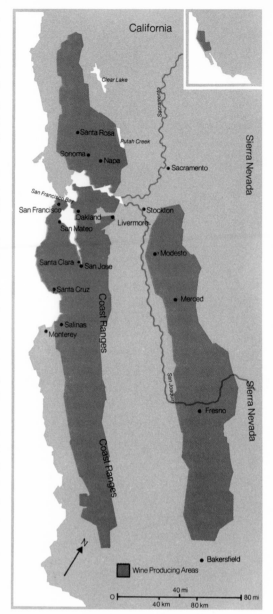

Maryland and Michigan. The main grape varieties are Concord, Fredonia, Isabella, Catawba, Delaware, Diana and Duchess. Various hybrid grapes are also grown, such as Alpha, Baco, Seibel and Seyve-Villard.

Wines made solely from native grapes, and those which are a blend of the product of native and hybrid grapes, have a pronounced flavour which is known in the United States as 'foxy'. This does not, mercifully, suggest that the wines taste as though the grapes have been trodden by foxes; the description probably owes its origin to the Fox grape, a variety that grows wild in several parts of the country. Some of these wines have merit, but they do not, in general, greatly appeal to serious wine drinkers. Wines made from hybrid grapes are generally much more satisfactory.

South America Wine is made extensively in South America, the biggest producer being Argentina, where the industry was developed chiefly by Italian immigrants. Many wines are good but in no way outstanding. Most of the production is red, but there is also white and rosé as well as a good deal of sparkling wine. The chief centre is the province of Mendoza. The Argentinians themselves are thirsty drinkers of their own wine products, ranking among the world's biggest per capita consumers. In consequence little is seen of Argentinian wine in the outside world.

Although Argentina is South America's biggest producer, the most meritorious wines of the whole of South America come from Chile. The tradition here has good French foundations, for when winemaking made its start on an appreciable commercial scale in the middle of the last century, the Chileans sensibly imported not only French vine cuttings, but French experts. The high quality of much of the wine today reflects this intelligent start.

The Cabernet grape produces red wine of exceptional quality, soft, smooth and with an excellent vinous flavour which is seldom found in even the better reds outside France. Some of these wines are decidedly superior to many of the more ordinary kinds of claret. The Pinot Noir is also grown, but not with such successful results.

The ubiquitous Riesling is another star performer in Chile. There has been some diminution of Riesling production lately because the grape is not a big producer and it was becoming increasingly expensive to utilise it. Other attractive whites are made from the Sauvignon, Pinot Blanc and Sémillon.

There are sound Government controls on Chilean wine production, which are an important factor in maintaining and promoting quality. The important areas include the Aconcagua and Maipo valleys.

North Africa Algeria, Morocco and Tunisia are all wine producers; Algeria, indeed, is one of the world's largest producers. North African wine has a somewhat tarnished reputation as an abundant and cheap commodity for filling out thin French ordinaires. This is what much of it continues to be used for, but not all North African wine necessarily deserves this fate. Algerian reds, in particular, are capable of no mean showing, and can improve considerably if kept in bottle for three or four years. The better qualities are grown on the slopes of the Atlas Mountains.

The general character of the reds from these three countries, however, can be summed up as dark, heady and rather coarse. Whites and rosés are also made but they are of no particular distinction.

With a Sparkle

Opposite Remuage *at Château Moncontour,*
Vouvray, on the Loire, where the best-known
non-Champagne sparkling wine of France is made,
using the méthode champenoise

A ll kinds of still wine, red, white and rosé, can be made to sparkle, and not a few of them are, with varying results. The choice ranges from de luxe brands of Champagne at dizzy prices down to fizzy vin ordinaire, which can often taste like still-fermenting grape juice with a spoonful of sugar thrown in. Between those two extremes there is a legion of bottles, Champagne and non-Champagne, many of which make very stylish drinking indeed.

The shortest definition of sparkling wine is that it is wine that has been made effervescent as a result of the presence of carbon dioxide in the bottle. The most laborious, and therefore the most costly, means of doing this is the Champagne method *(méthode champenoise)* in which a second fermentation takes place in the bottle. The short route to a not dissimilar, but less refined, result, is the Charmat process, in which the wine gets its secondary fermentation in closed tanks, and it is fair to describe sparkling wine made in this way as mass-produced wine. Yet another way of making wine sparkle is to pump carbon dioxide gas into it; such wines are not to be recommended.

The world at large is only too ready to trade on the fame of Champagne. In Spain, for example, bars list 'Champagne' at staggeringly low prices. But this is not Champagne; it is Spanish sparkling wine. Nothing from outside France, and indeed nothing from outside the province of Champagne, is entitled to call itself Champagne.

Not a few wines from elsewhere do, however, mention on their labels that they have been made by the méthode champenoise. There is nothing in the slightest illegitimate about this. It is open to anyone to adopt the laborious methods of Champagne, and many non-Champagne wines produced in this way are of an exceptionally high standard. And many very agreeable sparklers are made by the closed tank method. It cannot be said categorically that one method is necessarily always better than the other, for clearly there are other important factors to be taken account of, not the least of which is the quality of the wine that is being processed. But only a reckless vigneron would devote time, effort and money on using the méthode champenoise to make poor wine sparkle. In general non-Champagne sparkling wines made by the méthode champenoise have the edge on the tank-made product.

CHAMPAGNE

Champagne is universally accepted as the finest of sparkling wines. Made usually from a combination of red and white grapes, it can be dry, medium-dry or sweet, and sometimes it is rosé. Everything is in its favour: climate, soil, terrain all combine to make the perfect conditions for producing a polished dry white wine.

Up to the end of the seventeenth century the wines of Champagne were still and red. They did not keep well and they did not like to travel. In the 1660s the Champenois turned their hands to making white wine, which was not much of a success, being greyish, rather than white. But it was the beginning of sparkling Champagne, for it was seen to ferment for a second time as the weather became warmer.

It was Dom Pérignon, a monk at the Benedictine Abbey of Hautvillers, who exploited this phenomenon. As cellarmaster at the Abbey, to which job he was appointed in 1670, he became interested in the new white wine and the reasons for its secondary fermentation. He studied and experimented; he saw that the time to bottle the wine was in the spring following the vintage, when it became fizzy; he realised that if the bubbles were to be kept in the wine then the old-style bottle-stoppers made of pegs wrapped with oiled hemp would have to go, and he introduced corks, held in place with stout twine.

Over the years of experimentation Dom Pérignon's cellars were often awash with the wine from exploding bottles, but the monks found that in the bottles that did survive an astonishing transformation had taken place; the old, grey wine had become round, robust and fragrant, and it was, moreover, alive with waves of golden bubbles.

It was the start of success, but Dom Pérignon was not content to rest on his laurels. It was he who first appreciated the value of marrying the different growths of Champagne in a blend, using wines from different vineyards and from different years. It was he who foresaw the possibilities of tunnelling into the chalk and rock of the area to make perfect cellars for storing the wine.

Although a number of important developments have taken place across the years, the basic principles established by Dom Pérignon continue to be followed today. The first step after the pressing and the primary fermentation in casks is to blend the wines of different vineyards and varying qualities to form the cuvée, or store of wine.

The secondary fermentation occurs after the wine has been bottled, and it is at this stage that the carbon dioxide bubbles form and remain captive in the wine. Then the bottles are left undisturbed for a year or two so that the wine can mature.

Now comes a stage called *remuage*. During its long rest in the chalk cellars the wine gives off sediment which must be removed before the wine moves into the final stages of its preparation. Remuage is the initial part of the process of removing the sediment; the bottles are placed in special racks known as *pupitres*, at a slight angle, and each day a skilled man, a *remueur*, shakes each bottle and puts it back at a more acute angle. The object is to encourage the sediment to slide down the bottle and settle on the base of its temporary stopper. At the end of the process the bottles are completely inverted and the sediment will be where it is required for the next process, the *dégorgement*.

Still inverted, the bottle necks are dipped into a freezing mixture. The sediment and the small quantity of wine around it become ice. The cork is removed and the sediment is ejected as a frozen bullet.

Finally comes the *dosage*. A solution of Champagne and sugar syrup is added. Just how much sugar goes in depends on how sweet the wine is intended to be. The driest, *brut*, may have none, and the topping-up is done with unsweetened Champagne. But totally dry Champagne no longer has the popularity it once had, and brut may well have a small quantity of sugar syrup. *Extra sec* and *sec* will have a little more. *Demi-sec* will be well dosed with sugar syrup, and the rich *doux* even more so.

After this the bottles are sent back to rest again, for perhaps a year or more, before they are ready for the market.

Pink Champagne is made by allowing the skins of the black grapes to remain in contact with pressed grape juice at the time of the vintage.

Vintage Champagne is made only in particularly good years, which in the Champagne district means when there has been more sunshine than in a normal year. Although the label will show the vintage year the bottle may possibly contain some older wine; this is perfectly permissible, but is likely to be done only when the maker believes he can make an even better wine by doing so. The decision on whether or not to offer a vintage is entirely up to the maker. Vintage Champagne is usually firmer and has more decisive characteristics than non-vintage.

Non-vintage Champagne is simply the product of the vintages of a number of different years, blended. It forms by far the largest proportion of the output of the Champagne area.

De luxe brands are offered by many of the Champagne houses. They are made up of what the maker considers to be particularly good years. Some are blanc de blancs, which is Champagne made only from white grapes. It seems superfluous to add that the de luxe brands are among the more costly Champagnes.

Grandes marques These are the major Champagne houses, all of them famous; Veuve Clicquot, Heidsieck Dry Monopole, Krug, Pommery & Greno and Louis Roederer are examples. There are other smaller Champagne houses, many of them producing high class wines.

Although Champagne is rated the world's finest sparkling wine, it needs to be said that it is possible to buy indifferent Champagne. The word Champagne is not of itself an automatic guarantee of quality.

OTHER SPARKLING WINES
France Elsewhere in France there is a vast production of sparkling wines. Indeed, almost every wine-producing area makes some. The best-known is Vouvray, from the Loire valley. It is a rather fuller wine than non-vintage Champagne, and is never as dry as dry Champagne. The méthode champenoise is used in Vouvray, and it is also used to turn out quality sparkling wines in other districts of the Loire valley, notably Saumur and Mountlouis. Seysell, on the Rhône, makes an admirable clean, delicate sparkler which is as close to good non-vintage Champagne as anything outside the Champagne area is likely to get. Burgundy turns some of its red wines into sparklers, but these are not as successful as a pink one called Oeil de Perdrix, partridge eye.

Italy So far as the world at large is concerned, two Italian wines are memorable: Chianti and Asti spumante. Asti is the popular sparkling

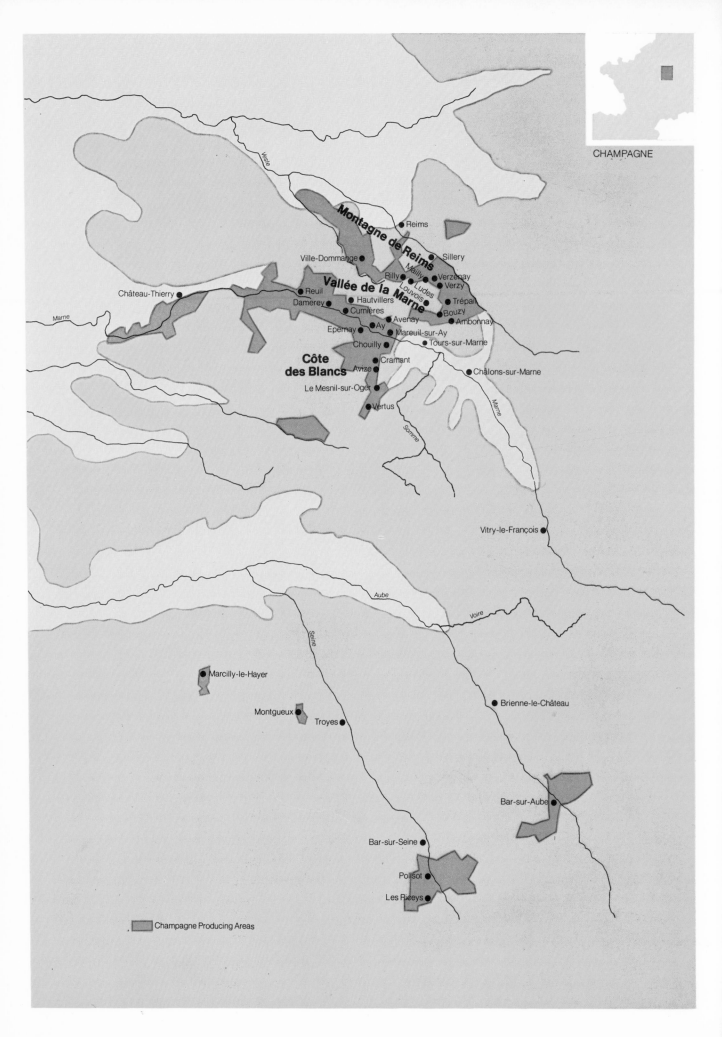

CHAMPAGNE

Montagne de Reims

Vallée de la Marne

Côte
des Blancs

Reims
Sillery
Ville-Dommange
Mailly
Verzenay
Rilly
Ludes
Verzy
Louvois
Château-Thierry
Reuil
Trépail
Damerey
Hautvillers
Bouzy
Cumières
Avenay
Ambonnay
Epernay
Ay
Mareuil-sur-Ay
Chouilly
Tours-sur-Marne
Cramant
Avize
Châlons-sur-Marne
Le Mesnil-sur-Oger
Vertus

Vesle
Marne
Somme
Marne

Vitry-le-François

Aube
Voire

Marcilly-le-Hayer

Seine

Brienne-le-Château

Montgueux
Troyes

Bar-sur-Aube

Bar-sur-Seine

Polisot

Les Riceys

Champagne Producing Areas

Top *The Abbey of Hautvillers, where Dom Pérignon, the chief cellarer, perfected the art of making Champagne at the end of the seventeenth century*

Above *Vats for the first fermentation at the Maison Moët & Chandon*

Left *Treading grapes in Champagne*

wine of Italy, made from the scented muscat grape, and having, in its best examples, all of the summery fruitiness of that grape.

The town of Asti is in Piedmont, in the extreme north-west corner of Italy. Not far away is Turin, better known for vermouth and engineering than for wine. Nearly all the wine made in the area is converted to spumante, either Asti spumante or Moscato d'Asti. Some of the makers use the méthode champenoise for their best wines.

Most of the sparkling wines from this area are sweet, although in recent years the trend towards drier wines has persuaded some of the makers to try their hand at less sweet wines, using Riesling or Pinot grapes. So far not many of these have been exported.

Sparkling wines are made in various parts of Italy, but none has achieved the popularity of Asti. Among those which are likely to have a good commercial future abroad are sparklers made in the South Tyrol.

Germany Sekt is what the Germans call sparkling white wine, and they have an enormous appetite for it. A nineteenth-century Berlin actor established the name: when playing Falstaff calling for his cup of sack he called for Sekt, which up until that time had been known as *Schaumwein*; but the word Sekt became a national joke, and the name stuck.

Some German sparklers are extremely good, and they are by no means confined to the most expensive, which can cost around the same price as a decent non-vintage Champagne, and are therefore not a particularly good buy. Plain Sekt need not, under German wine laws, necessarily be made from grapes grown in Germany, and some of the fizzy concoctions comprising partly German wine, partly imported wine, are unexciting.

The cheapest varieties of Sekt are best ignored. Better qualities will make good, clean drinking, but they are suitable as alternatives to Champagne or Vouvray only when their price is appreciably lower than the price of those wines.

Spain Here are produced quantities of sparkling wines which, price for price, offer better value than many German sparklers. They have no particular distinction, but simply offer good, straightforward drinking, usually medium rather than dry or sweet, at a modest price.

The United States California is one of the few new wine-growing areas of the world that is able to produce a creditable sparkling wine. Much of it is sold as Champagne, which must no doubt grieve the French; but in a country that is more conscious than most, in the matter of wine, of the difference between domestic and imported produce, one might suppose that the name-borrowing does not necessarily harm the sales of authentic Champagne.

Some of these wines use the grapes that are used in Champagne, and the méthode champenoise is also used. In general these wines are the best qualities. Some succeed in emulating at least a degree of the finesse of Champagne. Very few are truly dry in the way that brut Champagne is.

There is considerable production of sparkling wines in New York State. Some of them are decidedly agreeable, but since there is difficulty in growing traditional wine grapes in this part of the United States, American native vines are used extensively, with the result that the wines, while showing no lack of character, tend to taste somewhat perfumed.

Below *View of the Marne valley from Moët & Chandon's vineyards*

Right *Moët & Chandon vineyard workers celebrating the vintage*

A picker with a pair of épinettes in his hand, during the Champagne vintage

Filling Champagne casks with must for the first fermentation

In the Pink

Opposite *Wine storage domes at the company of José Maria da Fonseca at Vila Nogueira de Azeitão, Portugal – each dome holds 2636 hectolitres (58,000 gallons). The famous Lancers is produced here*

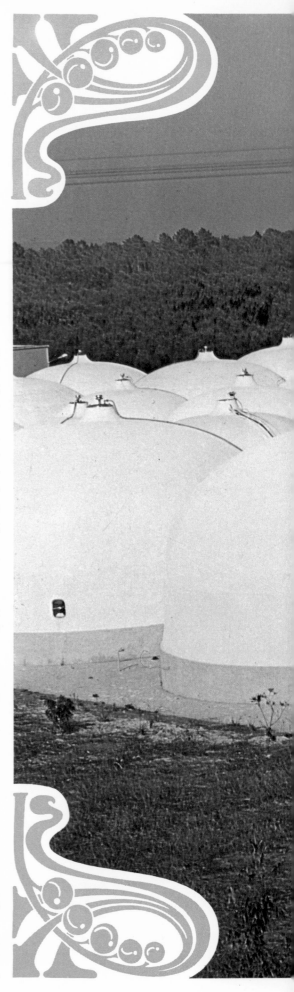

Rosé comes in all shades of pink, some of them dashing, some jolly, some rather serious. But rosé is an easy wine, a friendly wine, and one that is not to be taken very seriously. People drinking rosé should be – and have every right to be – more relaxed and convivial than people drinking almost any other kind of wine.

No-one prizes it highly. There is no fevered bidding and counter-bidding for it in the wine markets of the world. No-one has ever pronounced a rosé of any sort to be a *fine* wine, and no-one is ever likely to. It is, at its best, a likeable, pleasant wine. You can find plenty of people who do not rate rosé as a wine to be savoured, thought over, discussed, but you will find few who have a thorough-going dislike of it.

Prices, in consequence, are fairly modest by today's standards. The best of the rosés represent some of the best value for money on the wine merchant's shelves.

It is also adaptable. Some varieties are robust enough to get along famously with quite pungent food. This makes them exactly the right choice when you are pouring for people whose taste in wine is unknown. If, for example you suspect that one or more of your guests has a spitting dislike for red (and an uncommon number of people do, whether or not they are prepared to admit it) yet white simply will not match the lunch, then rosé is the stuff.

Rosé, however, has a great deal more merit to it than just a handy compromise for the unexpected guest. Much pink wine, decently chilled, makes delectable drinking of a lightweight kind when you need something in quaffable quantities to take the heat from your brow in a hot spring or a dusty summer. It can complement food, and even enhance food, provided it is not expected to contribute too much. It is not, somehow, a dinner wine, because dinner happens more often than not after nightfall, and after nightfall people are more thoughtful, and are inclined to more positive flavours than pink wine can ever offer. It is more of a daytime wine, because in the daytime it is more allowable to be flippant. And rosé is a flippant wine. Even the more solemn kinds of rosé are flippant when you get to grips with them.

Some of the best kinds are French. This does not mean, by a long chalk, that all French rosés are good, and that those from all other wine countries are, by contrast, second-rate. There are rosés from

France, as there are rosés from elsewhere, that are so sour they would be more at home sprinkled over a salad than in a wine glass, and others again that taste like liquified candy-floss – sweetly inoffensive, without the soul of a mouse. Rosé is enormously popular in the regions in which it is made, and especially in the United States.

France Tavel is not always the best known of French rosés, but it is the one with by far the best reputation. The vineyards, on the banks of the river Rhône, lie opposite Châteauneuf-du-Pape, and they are renowned only for their rosé. The wine is darker in colour than many other pink wines, is rather heady, and has a distinctive, rather suave flavour that makes it, if not a serious wine, then one that is a good deal less frivolous than a rosé is expected to be.

Tavel should be firmly dry, plump in fruitiness, and with a much more positively vinous flavour than one would expect to encounter in a demurely-tinted wine. It is well able to hold its own against assertive food flavours.

The Loire valley is a prolific producer of rosé wines, with Anjou, Touraine and Saumur among the principal districts. The one that is widely available in the United Kingdom is more often than not known simply as Anjou rosé. This will almost certainly be a meek, unexceptionable wine with some sweetness about it. But Anjou rosé Cabernet – wine made from the Cabernet grape – will be a less tender, more palatable wine, with much more fullness and a drier taste.

Provence is another big maker of pink wines. They are clean and strong, usually with a good scent. The vineyards around the small port of Cassis make one of the best pink wines, with all the good characteristics of Provençal rosé, but having more body than most others. Other good rosés come from the Provençal districts of Bandol and Bellet. Of branded Provence rosés Pradel is among the best known.

Rosé is made extensively elsewhere in France, Bordeaux being one of the principal producers. In Burgundy the village of Marsannay makes a pale, delicate rosé which has achieved considerable popularity in the United States. The Jura is a big producer, with strong tasting rosé that might persuade you to believe you are drinking a light red, and round the town of Arbois some delicate pinks are made, often with more than a hint of sweetness to them.

Germany Here are made some pink wines, at least one of which has lately been available in the United Kingdom. These are agreeable enough, but not special.

Switzerland This might be the last country in which one might expect to find a wine as unsolemn as rosé, but there it is, and very good it is, too. The wines of Neuchâtel are the most widely exported, and the pinks from this area are sprightly and fresh.

Portugal With the stupendous success of pink and pétillant wines, Mateus and Lancers, on the British and United States markets, anyone with a strip of land producing anything resembling a pétillant pink wanted to get in on the act. Few have succeeded, though there are still plenty of Portuguese pinks on the market. Most of them come from the Douro area, the home of port, and are amiable and anxious to please, but with barely any vinous character. Other Portuguese rosé wines of the non-pétillant variety are pleasant enough, if you have worked up a really sandy thirst.

Harvesting in a vineyard on the Loire. The spiked stick on the left of the picture is used to press the grapes into the plastic bin

Eastern Europe Both Hungary and Yugoslavia export quantities of pink wine. Hungary's is made from a little-known grape variety, the Kadarka, and is light and cooling. Yugoslavian rosé is more decisively flavoured and fruitier. Both are pleasant and cheap.

Italy Rosé is made all over Italy, but the best variety is grown in Lombardy, around Lake Garda, and is known as Chiaretto del Garda. It is a darker shade of pink than a typical rosé from France, and is light, lively and fresh, leaving a faint bitterness on the palate. Chiaretto del Lago d'Iseo is a similar wine.

In Tuscany, the House of Ruffino make Rosatello Ruffino, an attractive pink with good fragrance. A very popular variety is made in the Trentino-Alto Adige area, Lagarino Rosato. Another deep-coloured pink, it has a delicate build and a pleasing perfume.

Ravello rosés, from Campania, have a considerable export market. Again they are fairly dark in colour, and are usually middleweight with a tendency to sweetness.

Greece Greece makes rosé wines among her considerable wine output, but the only notable kind among them is pink retsina, which some people find more acceptable than white retsina because the more sturdy flavour of pink wine helps to keep at bay the flavour of resin.

The United States This is a large producer and consumer of pink wines, some of them made successfully from native grape varieties in New York State and Maryland, others from European varieties, notably the Grenache, in California. The Grenache is the grape grown in the Rhône valley for Tavel, and it has proved remarkably successful for making rosé in California. Some Californian Grenache rosés can, indeed, rival Tavel itself. Another grape of rather mysterious origin, the Zinfandel, which is the most widely cultivated grape variety in the whole of California, is also used to make agreeable pink wines.

The production of rosé has not gained such a firm foothold in most of the other newer wine-producing countries. There is some production in South Africa, with not a few very attractive varieties, and some in Australia. In general, however, there is not a big demand for such wines from export markets and they are rarely seen outside their country of origin.

Well Fortified

Opposite *In the vineyards of the Macharnudo area near Jerez de la Frontera. The mule carries porous amphoras of antique design which keep their contents cool by evaporation in the intense heat*

In various parts of Europe thriving industries have grown up to serve the British taste for sweet, fortified wines – some of which were invented by the British, and drunk by them, almost exclusively, for the best part of a couple of centuries.

With the exception of Spain, whose sherry trade continues to boom, the makers of these wines could be excused for feeling somewhat put out over being abandoned by the British. Even port, once known as 'the Englishman's wine', does brisker business in France these days than it does in Britain.

It may be that tastes will turn again to these wines – there are, indeed, indications that port is moving out of the doldrums on the British market, and Madeira has been making some headway towards a comeback. But Malaga, Marsala and Tarragona are largely forgotten wines.

PORT

Port can claim to be the world's greatest fortified wine. It was created by resourceful merchants at the beginning of the eighteenth century. Imports of French wine were debarred or hindered, but traders saw the prolific production of the Douro valley in Portugal as a likely alternative source of supply. The Douro wines were however very potent and rather disagreeable. They had to be made less potent and more palatable and the solution, found no doubt after many trials and errors, was to stop the fermentation by adding high-strength grape spirit. This made the wine less alcoholic and at the same time retained some of its natural sweetness.

This was the best thing that could have happened to the wine of the Douro valley. It launched an industry that was to establish an international trade, and its finest products were to become numbered among the world's most prized wines. The British and the Portuguese between them worked out a system of controls over every aspect of the wine-making process to ensure quality and authenticity, with the result that the wine became one of the best-protected against fraud and doubtful practices of any wine.

Ruby port Virtually all port with the exception of vintage port is a blend of the wine of different years to ensure continuity of style. The

136

main difference between the styles derives from the length of time a wine is given to mature. Ruby port is the shortest matured, lying in cask for perhaps only three or four years before being bottled. Ruby is full-bodied, robust and deep ruby in colour. It is the ordinaire of the port spectrum, bearing about as much resemblance to aged vintage port as does a plain Bordeaux rouge to a grand cru. But even the cheapest kind of ruby must achieve a respectable rating before it is allowed to leave Portugal.

Tawny port This spends longer in cask, as a general rule, than ruby, gradually taking on the brownish colour that gives it its name. The best, and most expensive, may mature in cask for ten years or more. Tawnies should be less sweet and lighter in body than rubies. Some of the oldest and finest can attain a peak of perfection approaching the flawless smoothness of a vintage port.

Tawnies can also be made by mixing white port with red, but the wine that is made by this method cannot show the gracefulness that characterises a well-aged tawny. For this reason it is best to avoid the cheapest of the tawnies.

Crusted port This is a blend of high-quality wines usually from different vintages. It has been called the poor man's vintage port, for like vintage it spends several years in cask and several more in bottle, and throws a crust within the bottle. The result is an elegant, well-balanced wine of some finesse, attributes that can be achieved only by considerable ageing.

White port White port is made from white grapes and made in much the same way as tawny. Some brands claim to be dry, but are seldom so in the accepted sense of the word. Well-chilled white port makes an agreeable aperitif.

Late-bottled port Late bottling is simply a means of speeding up the development of port. It ages faster in cask than it does in bottle, so in cask it stays for perhaps six or eight years instead of the two years for vintage port. The wines made thus have some of the characteristics of vintage port, though they are shallower, less decisive characteristics. Such wine does not throw a crust so that decanting is unnecessary.

Vintage port There is, of course, a vintage every year in the Douro valley, but it is only in a particularly fine year that a producer declares a vintage, and sets aside some of his wine which will be destined to become, say, Cockburn's 1967. Only the wine of the declared year can be used, though the use of wines from different *quintas* (wine farms) is allowable.

The decision as to whether to declare a vintage rests solely with the maker. It can happen that only one maker will decide in a particular year that his wine is going to be good enough to be designated a vintage; in other years all the makers may decide that their wine is good enough.

After two or three years in cask, vintage port is shipped abroad (usually to the United Kingdom) for bottling. It is then ready to go on to the market, but it will take anything from ten to thirty years before it is ready for drinking.

Vintage port starts life as a big, handsome wine. It acquires mellowness and softness only with age. The two constituents, wine and brandy,

Top The city of Porto seen across the Douro from Croft's port bodegas in Vila Nova de Gaia

Right Croft's Quinta da Roêda vineyard near Pinhão in the heart of the upper Douro valley port wine area

Right *The Douro valley just below Croft's Quinta da Roêda before the hydro-electricity barrages built in 1973 raised the river level*

Centre *In the patio of his sixteenth-century* palacio, *Palacio San Blas, next to the Domecq bodegas that fill the old centre of Jerez de la Frontera, stands Don José Domecq de la Riva. In his hand is a morning copita of pale golden La Ina, the fino sherry produced by his family. By Jerez custom he drinks this wine well chilled, as fino sherry is meant to be drunk*

Far right *Pipes of tawny port mature for years in wood in the Croft bodegas at Vila Nova de Gaia*

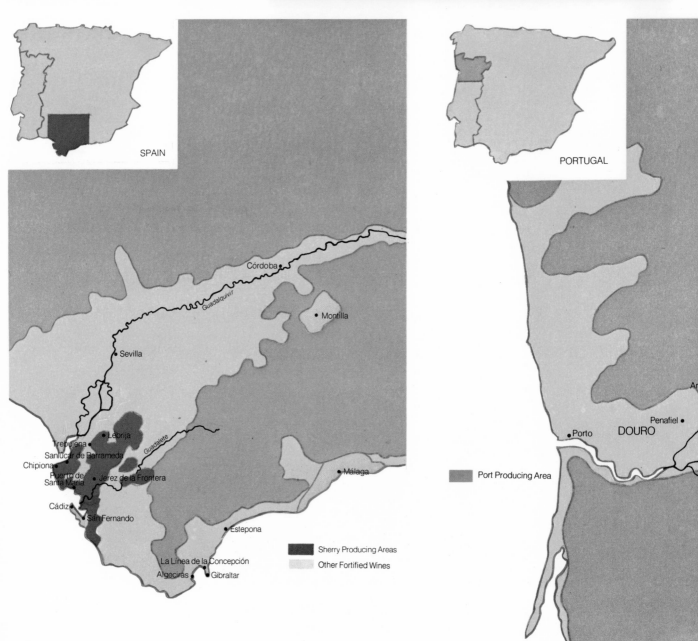

SPAIN

PORTUGAL

Córdoba

Guadalquivir

Montilla

Sevilla

Lebrija

Trebujena

Sanlúcar de Barrameda

Chipiona

Guadalete

Puerto de Santa María

Jerez de la Frontera

Málaga

Cádiz

San Fernando

Estepona

La Línea de la Concepción

Algeciras

Gibraltar

■ Sherry Producing Areas

▨ Other Fortified Wines

Porto

DOURO

Penafiel

Am

■ Port Producing Area

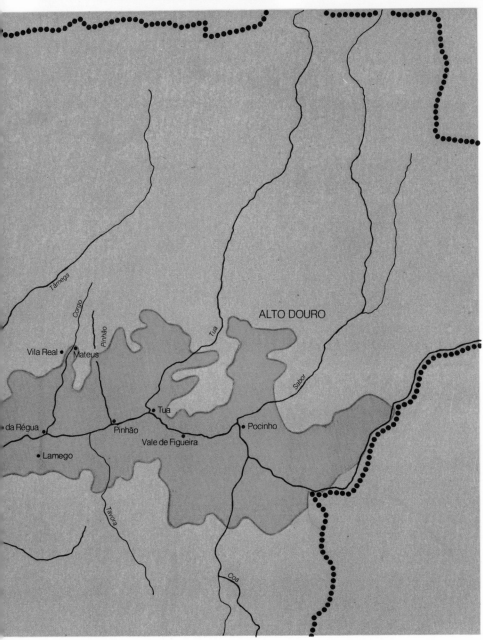

Tâmega

Corgo

Pinhão

ALTO DOURO

Tua

Sabor

Vila Real • Mateus

• Tua

da Régua • Pinhão • Pocinho

Vale de Figueira

• Lamego

Tavora

Coa

gradually draw together until they are in perfect harmony. None of the imperfections of youth remain. The result is smooth and delicate and infinitely agreeable.

Bottling in the Delaforce lodges at the historic entrepot of Vila Nova de Gaia opposite Porto across the Douro

SHERRY

Sherry is a blended and fortified wine that comes from a defined area in south-west Spain around the town of Jerez, to the anglicised rendering of which the wine owes its name. It is imitated in several parts of the world, sometimes successfully, sometimes less so; but real sherry is Spanish, the best of which cannot be equalled by the product of any other country.

It seems, on the face of it, the least complicated of wines. There are no vintage dates to worry about. It comes in sweet, medium or dry. Its storage and serving need no particular thought or effort.

But this simplicity is somewhat deceptive, and sherry has such a diversity of styles and varieties that it seems a gross over-simplification to give it a general, all-embracing label at all. There is about as much common ground between a crackling dry fino and a lusciously sweet cream sherry as there is between Chablis and Sauternes.

This range of differing sherry styles exists because sherry is one of those wines that owe at least as much to man as to nature. There is little element of chance in achieving the right end-result; it is achieved by blending, using wines of similar style but differing age, which is why there are no vintage dates to worry about.

Notwithstanding the variety of sherry types, there are only two main basic categories, *fino* and *oloroso*. Both start life as pale, dry wines, and if the blender is setting out to make a medium or sweet style he doses it with a secondary wine made from sweet grapes. Another secondary wine can be used for colouring.

There are some unusual features in sherry-making which, while they are not unique to sherry, play an important part in making it the distinctive wine it is. The first of these is a curious growth called *flor*.

After the grapes have been pressed in September the juice is taken to the *bodegas* (storage warehouses) where it ferments for several months before the initial fortification. Within a few weeks a white, not altogether attractive organic growth appears on the surface of the wine in some casks. This is known as *flor del vino*, a special kind of yeast.

The fact that it does not necessarily appear in all the casks (even in all casks holding wine from the same vineyard) is important. The wine in those casks in which it has failed to appear, or in which its growth has been checked by a dose of spirit, are destined to become oloroso. Those destined to become fino are allowed to develop for some years growing flor all the time.

The *solera* system is another notable feature of sherry making. At the centre of it is the oldest and most mature wine; moving out from the centre, graduated in order of seniority (and therefore of maturity) are perhaps six other wines, all of the same style.

The wine that is needed for bottling and shipping is drawn from the oldest cask. It is replenished with wine from the second oldest. That, in turn, is replenished with wine from the third oldest; and so on, until the youngest wine in the system is replenished with new wine. By contrast with the immense quantity of wine held in a solera, the quantity that is removed on each occasion is minute; thus the quantity of wine that finds its way into each scale of the solera is readily absorbed by the great sea of older wine, and in no way alters the taste and characteristics of the wine that is the end-product of the system. Consistency of style is the objective of the solera system.

Since vintage dates have no relevance for sherry, there is sometimes bafflement over the date sometimes shown on the label of various brands of sherry. However, a wine that is marked, for example, 'Solera 1850' is not claiming that all of the wine in the bottle actually dates from that time, merely that 1850 was the year when the solera from which that particular blend has been made was initiated, and that an 1850 wine is the oldest wine in the blend.

Once the wine has been drawn from the solera system, and the sediment removed, blending takes place. This creates a number of differing styles, including the two basic styles of fino and oloroso.

Fino sherries These are at the driest end of the sherry scale, light golden in colour and light but sometimes severe in the mouth. The Spaniards take their sherry unsweetened, but most of the finos designated for export have some degree of sweetening in them. Fino loses part of its freshness and aroma upon being bottled, and as little as two years after bottling it is likely to start to fade. It should therefore be bought as and when it is needed for drinking.

Manzanilla This is a fino that has been matured close to the sea, and from this experience acquires its peculiar salty tang. It is one of the few sherries that could accompany savoury food – perhaps at an informal meal of fresh prawns or shrimps served with brown bread and butter.

Amontillado The best amontillados are made by selecting promising finos to acquire age, colour and fullness in cask, and their most notable characteristic is an agreeable nutty flavour. The less costly varieties, however, are likely to have less age and to have added colour and sweetening, although some amontillado must be in them if they are to retain the essential nuttiness of this style.

Oloroso This is a dark, fairly heavy wine with a fat vinous flavour. Natural oloroso is dry, but most of those sold outside Spain have some sweetness.

Cream sherry This is an oloroso with considerable sweetening. The best known example is Harvey's Bristol Cream, a blend of very old olorosos, amontillados, and sweetening wine.

Old-bottled sherry Once it has been bottled, sherry is ready for instant drinking. But oloroso, if it is given an opportunity to acquire bottle-age, can show a distinct development, becoming drier and assuming a distinctive nose and flavour. The better kinds of amontillado can also be developed in this way.

Montilla This wine is a close cousin of sherry, but may not be described as sherry since that name is confined to the wines of the Jerez area, and Montilla is made more than 150 kilometres away, near Córdoba. It can be sweet or dry, fortified or unfortified, but the best of the Montilla wines are the natural finos, light and bone-dry. They are made to be drunk young, and they will diminish quite soon once the bottle has been opened.

MADEIRA

Madeira is one of the most versatile of the fortified wines. It can be served as an aperitif, as a soup wine, as a dessert wine or as an after-dinner wine. It is also highly individual, with a unique flavour, and by today's standards it offers exceptionally good value for money.

The most distinctive feature of Madeira is its curious smoky after-taste. This is derived partly from the soil and climate of the island of Madeira, but chiefly from the 'cooking' process to which it is subjected, and which is an important stage of the wine-making process. The wine is put into a 'hot room' and heated to a temperature of 32–60°C. (90–140°F.) for several months before being fortified with spirit and matured in wood.

There are seldom vintage dates on Madeira bottles today. When a bottle bears a date it is the date of the oldest wine in the blend, for the Madeirans use the solera system (described in the previous section on sherry) under which old wines are topped up with new.

There are four main styles. All take their names from the grape varieties used to make them.

Sercial The driest. It is pale amber in colour and has a slightly bitter flavour. It makes a particularly attractive aperitif and is also the style to choose for serving with soup.

Verdelho Nearly as dry, but tends to be plumper in body. It can be drunk at the beginning or the end of a meal.

Malmsey The English rendering of the grape name Malvasia. It is deep-bodied, rich and soft. Its place is as a dessert wine.

Bual This is also a dessert wine, but it has less richness to it than Malmsey. Its principal merit over Malmsey is that it is usually rather cheaper.

Rainwater This is a sub-style developed mainly for the United States market, which has long appreciated Madeira wines. It is fairly light and

Palomino grapes being picked in the
Macharnudo area near Jerez de la Frontera

dry and is the result of blending wines made from Sercial and Verdelho grapes.

Port maturing in casks in the Delaforce lodges at Vila Nova de Gaia

OTHER FORTIFIED WINES

Port, sherry and Madeira are the world's most famous fortified wines. But wines of this sort are made in many countries, some of them having been, in their day, as renowned as the big trio are now, others having been developed in the newer wine-producing countries. For the most part they are sweet dessert wines, although dry sherry-type wines are made, notably in South Africa, Australia, Cyprus and the United States.

Marsala This is the main dessert wine of Italy, made in the north-west of Sicily, and taking its name from the name of a town in that area. It is a dark, assertively flavoured wine, with a scorched taste, not unlike that of Madeira. The best varieties are good, inexpensive after-dinner drinking. There is a fairly dry variety, called Virgin, which is remarkably good value as an aperitif. There are also various Marsala concoctions, of which the best-known is Marsala all'uovo, a combination of egg yolk, wine and spirit – a king of bottled zabaglione, but no bad pick-me-up

Malaga Like Marsala, this is a near-forgotten wine in the English-speaking world. The Germans have a great fondness for it and provide its chief market. It has a vast aroma and bouquet of raisins, and is one of the least costly of the fortified dessert wines. It comes from the area around the town of that name in Andalucia. The best-rated kind is made in a manner similar to that used in Hungary for making Tokay, and is known as Lagrima.

Tarragona Another Spanish wine, once known in the United Kingdom as 'poor man's port', it comes from the area south of Barcelona. It is a

thick, deeply-coloured, very sweet wine, but has no special attributes over and above its usually-moderate price.

Moscatel de Setúbal The port of Setúbal lies some thirty kilometres south of Lisbon, making sweet fortified wine by methods similar to those used for making port, but with a wholly different result. Setúbal is one of the less concentrated of sweet fortified wines, and one that has been recently bottled has an engaging perfume of fruit.

Port- and sherry-styles Outside the Douro valley and the area of Jerez there is vast production of port-styles and sherry-styles. Among the port-styles, while some perfectly agreeable wines are made, there is nothing to compare with authentic port, although some of the better port-styles from South Africa and Australia are often equal to, and sometimes surpass, the plainest kinds of authentic port.

Makers of sherry-type wines have been more successful in capturing the character of the genuine article. In South Africa, notably, a large range of excellent sherries is made, often offering better value for money than the humbler wines from Jerez. Especially successful are South African finos. One important factor in the general high quality of South African sherries is the similarity of climate and soil between Paarl, the centre of South African wine-making, and Jerez. Another factor is the considerable care the South Africans have lavished on perfecting their sherries. Wines have been produced by the solera system for only about thirty-five years.

The wine-makers of Cyprus, encouraged initially by the British administration and subsequently by the Government of the Republic of Cyprus, produce an extensive range of sherries. The sweet varieties, which so far have been the most commercially successful, lack the finesse of well-made sweet Spanish sherries, but they are not without appeal. After considerable efforts one or two good dry sherries are being made.

José Ignacio Domecq, director of Pedro Domecq, S.A., creates a sherry blend in the laboratory adjoining his office. The measure he uses represents a butt of sherry. A butt contains 500 litres (110 gallons), or 40 jarras (the standard stainless steel jugs or cannisters used in the bodegas of Jerez), each jarra being equivalent to 12·5 litres (2¾ gallons). Señor Domecq is known in Jerez for his remarkable knowledge of the wines stored in Spain's largest bodegas, the property of his family since 1730

Sauve & Spirited

*Opposite Checking samples for blending at the
International Distillers and Vintners whisky complex
at Blythswood near Glasgow in Scotland*

All over the world people are distilling – separating the alcohol in any alcoholic liquid by applying heat. Anything can form the body of the alcoholic liquid: fruit, sugar, grain, rice, vegetables. Distillation is no more than a means of converting certain raw materials into beverages of high alcoholic strength; it is a manufacturing process, with no more magic about it than that.

But some spirits have gained world renown for their finesse. Cognac is one, Scotch whisky another. There are other kinds of brandy and other kinds of whisky, but all of them are admitted, except by their closest devotees, to be followers in the field of spirits. There is white rum and medium-weight rum and dark, darkly-flavoured rum, all of them with their following. There is London gin and Plymouth gin and genever, and variations of one kind or another on almost any kind of spirit you care to think of. Everyone has his favourite, and there is little deep, thoughtful discussion of spirits as there is of wine. But spirit-fanciers tend to be more dogmatic than wine drinkers.

BRANDY

Brandy is among the most widely-made spirits, for it is a product of wine, and every wine-producing country makes some. The word is understood, in England, to relate to French brandy, usually Cognac. It originates from the words 'burnt wine'.

Cognac This brandy comes from the Charente district in western France. In Germany German brandy is often referred to as Cognac; in Spain, Spanish brandy. None of these, however, is Cognac; they are simply brandies, borrowing, for the sake of convenience, the name of the most prestigious member of their family. The great delicacy and poise of a good Cognac is inimitable.

The Cognac most commonly encountered is three-star, which indicates a maker's standard style. The age of a Cognac is one of the most important factors in its make-up. A three-star brandy will generally be about five years old.

One stage higher is VSOP. The initials stand for Very Superior Old Pale, although the second word is sometimes said to be 'special' or, more rarely, 'soft'. But the precise wording is not important; VSOP is widely understood to mean a better brandy than a three-star, because

it will have had more barrel-age, possibly up to twenty years.

After this comes a range of Cognacs, usually made in relatively small quantities, with more barrel-age than VSOP, or made from older or better quality wine, or all of these things. Some are called liqueur brandies, others 'special' or 'reserve'. The prime quality from the house of Hennessy is called XO. In general the price of these special qualities is considerable, while the difference between their character and that of VSOP is not massive.

Napoleon brandy is simply a style of Cognac, usually approximating to that of VSOP. Cognac, like other spirits, evaporates in cask, and a cask that had remained unrenewed by later Cognac since Napoleon's time would have run dry years ago. It is by no means impossible to find brandy that was bottled in Napoleon's time, but brandy does not improve in bottle; it can, indeed, deteriorate, if the cork should shrink. So 'Napoleon' should be recognised merely as a style, not as an indication of age, and cobwebbed bottles that claim to be Napoleon brandy should be rejected.

Armagnac This is the closest kinsman in the brandy world to Cognac in terms of quality. The best of it is better by far than the plainer kinds of Cognac. It is, by and large, less subtle and more assertively flavoured than Cognac; it is also, usually, somewhat cheaper. The three-star, VSOP, and special-quality descriptions apply in Armagnac as they do in Cognac.

'Pure French Grape Brandy' This is brandy made anywhere in France that is not entitled to a Cognac or an Armagnac appellation. It varies enormously in quality, but it is as a rule less pungently-flavoured than brandies from most other wine-producing countries. This is the stuff to drink with dry ginger, or to convert into brandy sour or brandy julep, rather than honest three-star cognac, which will be wasted in such concoctions.

Marc Marc is the distillate of husks of grapes and residual matter after wine has been made. It can be produced anywhere. In Italy and in California it is known as *grappa*. The taste for it is an acquired one; at first encounter it can have all the appeal of varnish. The lightest, and usually most acceptable, kinds are made in white-wine producing areas.

WHISKY
Whisky (whiskey in Ireland and America) is made in various parts of the world, but there is no real argument that the best of it comes from Scotland, Ireland, the United States and Canada. All are made of grain of one kind or another – barley, rye, wheat, corn or maize. All have their own special character, depending not only on the kind of grain used but on differing production processes, the kind of wood in which they are aged (sherry casks are widely used) and – an important consideration – on the nature of the water used.

Scotch whisky As it is known throughout the world this is a blend of two different kinds of whisky, malt and grain. Malt is made only from malted barley, an ingredient that is produced by wetting the barley to release the sugar or maltose in it, after which the barley is dried over a peat fire, giving the end product its distinctive smoky flavour. Grain

Distillery manager Mr. R. N. Arthur with Mr. J. Flemming, testing The Glenlivet after many years in the wood, at the Glenlivet distillery, perhaps the most famous malt distillery of all

whisky is made by a much more rapid process, using maize and barley, with the distillation carried out in a patent still, which is considerably more productive than the pot still used for malt.

Grain whisky has little commercial following in its own right; it is made for blending with malt, which gives it body and depth of flavour. A typical blend is likely to contain six parts of grain to four of malt, but obviously there are endless permutations for making the end-product light, by using less of the heavily-flavoured malt, or more 'peaty', by using more. Standard blends, however, do not vary in this way; their flavour, having established its own market, is constant.

There are various de luxe versions of blended whisky, just as there are de luxe versions of Cognac brands. These whiskies will be blended from component whiskies that are older and more mellow than those used in the standard blends – perhaps twelve years old, compared with five years for the standard blends.

Single malt whiskies are those produced by one distillery only, and remain unblended. They are heavier than blends, fairly pungent, and are gaining popularity as after-dinner drinks. The finest of them are said to come from distilleries in the vicinity of the river Spey, but there are more than ninety malt distilleries in Scotland.

Irish whiskey This is made by the same process as Scotch whisky, but there are some important differences. It is distilled three times, as against twice for Scotch. The malted barley is dried over coke or anthracite fires, instead of over peat. And as a rule it has a much larger proportion of malt in its make-up than Scotch; this can be around eighty per cent malt to twenty of grain. Usually the whiskey is of a greater age than that of standard brands of Scotch, for Irish law requires whiskey to be at least five years old before it is sold to the public, whereas the age requirement for Scotch is three years.

Some Irish whiskeys are aged for over twelve years, and make very smooth drinking indeed. The characteristic aroma and taste of Irish whiskey is very much more pungent than that of Scotch.

Bourbon This whiskey takes its name from the county of that name in Kentucky, where it originated in the colonial days of America. There are Bourbon distilleries now in many parts of the United States, but Kentucky remains the centre of Bourbon distilling.

Bourbon is made from a fermented mash of grain of which at least fifty-one per cent must be maize. The minimum age of Bourbon must be four years, and the ageing is done in barrels which have been charred on the interior. 'Straight' Bourbon is one that has been blended with other Bourbons, and it will have a more decisive aroma and flavour than blended Bourbon, which is the result of adding neutral grain spirit.

Rye whiskey Rye is made from grain of which at least fifty-one per cent must be rye. As in the case of Bourbon there is 'straight' rye and blended rye, and the ageing is done in charred barrels. The flavour is a heavy one, and the difference between rye and Bourbon is not unlike that between Scotch and Irish. The main centres of distillation in the United States are Maryland and Pennsylvania. Canadian rye whiskey has established a worldwide reputation; it has a distinctive lightness of body which sets it aside from other rye whiskeys.

*Below The House of Martell maintains a stock of
very old Cognacs for blending purposes in a special
cellar called, appropriately enough, Paradis*

*Bottom One of the earliest documents in the
possession of the House of Martell, dated 1723.
The firm was founded in 1715 when Jean Martell
left Jersey and settled in the Charente district of
France*

Right *Knockando-Glenlivet distillery on the river Spey in Morayshire, Scotland. This distillery was built in 1898 and with its pagoda-shaped roof over the kiln is typical of Highland malt whisky distilleries, which are often in remote settings in the hills*

Below A *spirit safe at Chivas Regal's malt distillery in Keith, Scotland*

OTHER SPIRITS

Gin Gin is made mostly from grain, but molasses spirit is sometimes used. It takes its name from the French word *genièvre* (juniper), the berries of which plant are one of the principal flavouring agents. Other flavourings may include coriander, angelica and almonds. Every gin-maker has his own formula for flavouring, and it is from this that each brand of gin takes its own special characteristics.

London dry gin, although it originated in London, need no longer today signify anything more than a style of gin; it can be produced in any part of the world, and the only expectation of it should be that it is unsweetened.

Hollands gin, or genever, is made by a process which retains some of the flavouring of the original grain in the end-product. Its taste is therefore heavier than that of most other varieties, and there is some oiliness about it.

Vodka This was once the drink of the Russians, Poles, Estonians and others of those parts of Europe; now it is made and drunk practically everywhere. It can be distilled from anything that will not impart a flavour to the distillate, but grain is usually the base. The objective is to make a clean, unflavoured spirit, although some vodkas with a flavouring of, for example, lemon or aniseed, are made.

Rum Rum uses sugar cane as its base. Sometimes this is in the form of juice from the cane; more often it is molasses, a by-product of the sugar-making process. Most of it originates in the Caribbean area, although any part of the world that is capable of producing sugar cane can produce rum, and in some instances molasses is exported from the Caribbean for rum production in other countries.

There are three principal varieties: the darkly-flavoured, richly heavy rums of which Jamaican and Guyanan rums are notable examples; medium-weight rums from such producers as Haiti, Trinidad and Barbados; and the lighter rums of Cuba and Puerto Rico, among others. White rum, that is colourless rum, usually with little flavour, has become popular in the last few years and makes a good base for long, mixed drinks.

Rum, like other spirits, will not improve once it has been bottled, but there are some rums which have been well aged in barrel, for perhaps fifteen years, and so take on a special elegance. They are suitable for serving as an alternative to brandy or liqueurs at the end of a meal.

Fruit brandies Fruit brandies, or *eaux de vie,* are distilled all over the place, but the most famous of them come from France and Germany. The great eau de vie of Normandy is Calvados, made from fully ripe apples and deriving its name from the town of Calvados, the centre of the Normandy apple-growing industry. The best Calvados will have six years at least in cask before it is bottled. Like other fruit brandies it is unsweetened and is for sipping at the end of a meal, served in a brandy glass. The equivalent in the United States is applejack.

Large quantities of plums are made into brandy. Those made from blue plums are known as Quetsch, those made from yellow plums as Mirabelle. In the Balkans plum brandies are known as Slivovitz.

In France, Germany and Switzerland pears are used to make a very

Ploughing malt at Benriach distillery, near Elgin, Morayshire

agreeable eau de vie known as Poire William. And Kirsch, which uses cherries, is extensively made in these countries and elsewhere. Other fruits, with the names of the spirit made from them, are raspberry (Framboise), strawberry (Fraise), and blackberries (Mûres sauvages).

Since everything that is fermentable will make a base for spirits, in different parts of the world all kinds of fruits, vegetables and grains *are* used, and the spirit spectrum is a vast one. Many of them, like the akvavit of Scandinavia, are little more than variations on straightforward spirits like gin and vodka, with different flavourings or no flavouring whatsoever. There are a few exceptions. Tequila is distilled from the juice of the maguey plant in Mexico. It has considerable popularity in the United States. And in Japan rice is the basis for Saké, a colourless spirit usually served warm.

Flavoured & Flighty

Man's ingenuity knows no limits when it comes to ways of dressing up alcohol to make it more tempting. Not infrequently it turns out to be far from tempting. The Italians, in particular, have some very good and some very bad ideas about doing things to wines and spirits to convert them into exciting patent drinks. The motive, no doubt, is that because there is so much wine in Italy any man who can devise a way of selling more of it deserves his just rewards.

Vermouth One of the most respectable and oldest-established of these 'manufactured' drinks is vermouth. Both the Italians and the French are good at making it, the special skills of the Italians being in making sweet vermouth, and those of the French in the drier varieties. Many other wine-producing countries make it, for all it amounts to is fortified wine that has been flavoured. The chief flavouring agent is wormwood, from the German rendering of which, *Wermut,* the drink derives its name.

Vermouth, like other kinds of flavoured wine, originated as a means of turning undrinkable wine into something palatable. It ceases to be recognisably wine; it becomes something else – vermouth, a drink in its own right, embracing not just the original wine, but wormwood, quinine, coriander, camomile, or other things the manufacturer may have in his formula. In general, the base wine is the plainest and cheapest available. Much of that used in Italian vermouth comes from the south and from Sicily; in France the great vin ordinaire area of the Midi is the main source.

Although Italian vermouth is universally regarded as the sweet variety, and French as the dry, both countries in fact make both kinds. And today names that are traditionally associated with one country or the other produce vermouth outside their homelands: Cinzano, for example, one of the most famous of Italian producers, has factories not only in Turin, the traditional centre of the vermouth industry in Italy, but in the United States and Australia.

The typical vermouth of Italy is dark red and sweet. That of France is white, fairly dry and much lighter. A comparative newcomer is bianco, which confuses the conventional scheme of things by being white and sweet – heavily sweet, in fact, but usually agreeably perfumed and an attractive enough party drink, provided it has been well chilled.

One other kind of vermouth is worth special note. This is Chambéry, made in France close to the border with Italy, and using light wines from the Alpine hillsides, and with a lighter infusion of herbs. It is one of the driest vermouths you will find, and one with the least assertive flavour.

Close cousins of vermouth are a great range of patent aperitifs. The most famous, perhaps, is Dubonnet, originating in France but now also manufactured in the United States. The most familiar variety is red, but a white version is also made. Both are sweet, but have an after-taste of bitterness derived from quinine and bark. Saint Raphaël and Byrrh are proprietary brands of much the same nature. Lillet is white, based on white wine and brandy, and is drier and less full-bodied than most of the others.

Then there are others which, to judge by their taste, lean more heavily on quinine for their flavouring. Among them is a notable Italian brand, Punt e Mes, which is probably a legitimate vermouth but is so distinctive that it sets itself apart. The flavour is at once sweet and bitter. Elsewhere in Italy quinine is used to flavour wines like Barolo which one might have imagined would have been eminently marketable without any additive. In Spain some sherry is also given a dose of quinine, and is then known as sherry kina.

Other kinds of wine-based aperitif abound. Two of the most noteworthy are Pineau des Charentes, made in the Cognac region of France from local grapes and dosed with young brandy, and ratafia, a rather musty-tasting aperitif based on wine usually from Champagne or Burgundy. Both, in common with most French aperitifs, are sweet. There are also many other fortified French wines, mainly from the south, which are drunk in France as aperitifs.

Spirit-based aperitifs This is stronger stuff. The most celebrated of them all is pastis, the aperitif of Marseille, with a dominating flavour of aniseed. Pastis is a member of a considerable family; in Greece and Cyprus it is ouzo; in the Middle East some kinds of arrack are not unlike pastis. All of them are descendants of absinthe, a potent spirit flavoured with anise and wormwood, which was banned in France at the start of the 1914–18 war, and subsequently by most other countries, because of its devastating effects on the nervous system, which were said to lead to blindness, madness and other afflictions.

The best-known brands of French pastis are Pernod, Ricard and Berger. They all need to be diluted with chilled water, which gives them a deceptively milky-mild appearance. In fact they are normally stronger than regular spirits, and need to be approached with caution.

One other notable spirit-based aperitif is Pimm's, made in England and based on gin. The formula is secret, but the drink is a very agreeable one with the addition of carbonated lemonade. Once there were varieties based on whisky, brandy, rum, rye and vodka, but these have disappeared and only the gin-based version remains.

Bitters Bitters are both for drinking for pleasure and for drinking medicinally. One of their most important roles in the drinking-for-pleasure category is as components of mixed drinks. One of their most important roles in the medicinal category is as hangover relievers.

Campari is the best-known of the bitters that are used as aperitifs. It is a magnificently red-coloured drink, made in Italy and flavoured, among others things, with orange peel. It is at its best served as a long drink with the addition of soda water, but is also an essential component of several cocktails, notably Negroni.

Amer Picon is French, dark and very bitter. There is wine and brandy in it, and a good dose of quinine, as well as orange peel and various herbs. It needs to be iced and watered, and most people find it more agreeable if some cassis or grenadine has been added, to give it some sweetness.

Orange bitters and peach bitters are both used for flavouring mixed drinks. Both are powerfully flavoured; a few drops will suffice. Sherry with a few dashes of orange bitters tossed in once had a vogue.

Angostura is another bitters used for flavouring, most of it probably going to provide the pink in pink gin. But it can flavour anything; one school of thought believes that it enhances shepherd's pie. Angostura is rum-based and made in Trinidad.

Underberg (German) and Fernet Branca (Italian) are both widely used as pick-me-ups, although they can serve as aperitifs. In Italy it is common to down a glass of Fernet Branca at the end of a long, well-wined meal; you anticipate the hangover and the stomach upset, and this constitutes avoiding action. It can be remarkably effective.

All of these highly-flavoured, somewhat exotic drinks have countless permutations and brand-names; probably every country in the world has some recipe for a speciality, whether it is an appetite-sharpener or a reviver. There is a variety called Cynar, which is made from Jerusalem artichokes. Suze is a popular brilliant yellow aperitif made in France from the gentian. And there is in Siberia and the Caucasus a drink called *kumiss*, which is made from fermented mare's milk. . . .

Sticky Endings

Liqueurs they are called in the United Kingdom, cordials in the United States, but the best term of all is the French one, which is *digestifs*. At least this gives you the comforting feeling that you are not merely drinking for pleasure, at a stage, more often than not, after you have already had a number of pleasurable drinks; but that what you are drinking is actually going to do you good.

A liqueur is a sweetened and flavoured spirit. Sometimes the word is applied to well-matured brandies and whiskies, but these are not liqueurs in the recognised sense, since they have no added sweetness. And some wine merchants, no doubt for the sake of convenience, list such drinks as akvavit, bitters, flavoured vodkas and fruit brandies under the heading of 'liqueurs', where they have no business to be. Everyone's expectation of a liqueur is that it will combine a compelling flavour with a soothing sweetness, and that is what it ought to be.

Throughout the history of alcoholic beverages people have used aromatic herbs and plants as a flavouring. Sometimes these ingredients had the express purpose of converting wine into a medicine; sometimes the purpose was to mask deficiencies in wine. Liqueurs as they are known today almost certainly had their origin as medicines, and there are still some which were first compounded by monks in the Middle Ages for this use. It seems probable that some of these early liqueurs had not a little of the generally disagreeable flavour that is associated with present-day medicines, for it was not until the nineteenth century that exotic spices and sugar became widely available to enhance their flavour.

There are three broad categories of liqueurs. Herb liqueurs are flavoured with herbs. Crème de Menthe is one that is made with the flavouring of only a single herb, mint. But many herb liqueurs use an immense variety of herbs; Chartreuse, for example, needs 126 different plants in its manufacture. Peel liqueurs are made mostly with citrus fruit, and depend on the flavour of orange or lemon for their dominating characteristic. Fruit liqueurs can be flavoured with almost any kind of fruit. Cherry brandy is probably the best known example. Bananas, raspberries, blackcurrants, peaches and almonds are among a wide range of other flavours.

What all these varieties have in common is, of course, alcohol. It may be brandy, whisky, rum, fruit spirit or grain spirit. The purest spirits make the finest liqueurs. And in addition to flavouring there has to be a sweetening agent, which is likely to be sugar or honey.

Several methods are used to bring the spirit and the flavouring together, but the main methods are infusion and percolation. In the former the flavouring agents are steeped in spirit until their colour and flavour have merged with the spirit, which is then redistilled to perfect the marriage.

Percolation involves passing alcohol vapours through the flavouring agents. This process is carried out in apparatus that is not unlike a coffee percolator, and the principle is the same.

There are countless kinds of liqueur, from the crude and fiery to honeyed nectar. Not all of them, by any means, live up to the reputation that liqueurs have for being dizzily alcoholic, but some are potent indeed, and need to be treated with caution.

Two liqueurs can justifiably claim a wider fame than any of the others. Both are French and both have associations with religious orders. They are Benedictine and Chartreuse.

Benedictine This was first compounded around 1510 by the monks of the Benedictine abbey at Fécamp, Normandy. The abbey was destroyed during the French Revolution, and the manufacture of the liqueur came to a halt. The recipe, however, came into the possession of M. Alexandre Le Grand, who restarted production in the 1860s. Although manufacture is still based at Fécamp, the business has no connection with any religious order. Each bottle, however, carries the letters DOM – Deo Optimo Maximo (To God most good, most great).

Yellowy-green in colour, the liqueur is flavoured with various plants, herbs and peel. The base is brandy. It is said that no more than three people at any one time know the complete formula.

B & B is Benedictine and brandy. It became known to the makers of Benedictine that people had taken to breaking the sweetness of the liqueur by adding brandy to it. So they made matters simpler for those with drier tastes by preparing and bottling such a mix.

Chartreuse Unlike Benedictine, this liqueur is still in the hands of the religious order which originally compounded it. The main ingredients are brandy, herbs and plants, though like so many other liqueurs, the recipe is a secret. Two strengths are made, the highest one being green in colour, the weaker, which happens also to be rather sweeter, being yellow.

The Carthusians are said to have been given the formula in the early 1600s, and to have subsequently made their own modifications to it. It was only in 1848, when a group of French army officers were present at the monastery in Grenoble and had an opportunity to drink the liqueur, that its existence became known to the outside world.

In 1903, religious orders were outlawed in France and the monks re-established themselves at Tarragona, Spain, where they continued to produce the liqueur. Their trade-mark was confiscated by the French authorities and a number of bad imitations of Chartreuse appeared on the market. This commercial setback was, however, overcome, and since their return to France in the 1930s the monks have carried on production at both Grenoble and Tarragona.

Other liqueurs

Apricot liqueurs are among the most pungently perfumed of the liqueurs. Most are made by macerating fresh apricots with grape brandy.

Aurum Herbs, oranges and old brandy are the principal ingredients of this Italian proprietary liqueur, made at Pescara.

Calisay comes from Catalonia. It has a slightly bitter after-taste suggesting the presence of barks in its composition.

Cherry brandy is one of the most popular of liqueurs, and Cherry Heering the most popular brand. It is made in Denmark by the firm of Peter Heering. Some of the cherry stones are used in the manufacturing process, with the result that Cherry Heering is not as fulsomely sweet as many of its rivals. Another excellent cherry brandy is made in England by the firm of Grants, using English-grown morella cherries.

Cointreau is a proprietary liqueur made at Angers, France, by the Cointreau family. It belongs to the curaçao (orange-flavoured) branch of liqueurs. Colourless, it has an attractively light finish and it is not penetratingly sweet.

Cordial Médoc originates, as its name suggests, in the Bordeaux area. It uses both wine and brandy, and various herbs give it an agreeably aromatic flavour.

Crème de Banane is made by macerating ripe bananas in spirit. The flavour and bouquet of bananas are, to say the least, positive.

Crème de Cassis Blackcurrants and grape brandy are the chief ingredients. The liqueur is sweet and has a highly fruity flavour. One of its uses is to make kir, an immensely refreshing summer drink consisting of a dash of crème de cassis in a glass of chilled, dry white wine.

Crème de Fraises and Crème de Fraises des Bois are tantalising fruit liqueurs, one made from strawberries, the other from wild strawberries.

Crème de Menthe is one of the most extensively produced liqueurs, and one of the most popular. The best known variety is identifiable by its scintillating green colouring, but there is also a white variety. The mint most commonly used in its preparation is a member of the same herb family as garden mint.

Curaçao is a generic name for a wide range of liqueurs using oranges as their flavouring. The name was originally applied only to liqueurs made with oranges from the Dutch Caribbean island of Curaçao.

Drambuie is the most famous of a number of liqueurs made in Scotland and using Scotch whisky as their base. Other ingredients are herbs and heather honey. Legends abound in the liqueur world; the one that concerns Drambuie is that after the defeat of the rebels in 1745, Mackinnon of Strathaird gave shelter to Prince Charles Edward; in his gratitude the Prince gave Mackinnon the recipe for Drambuie, which continues to be made by his descendants today.

Forbidden Fruit is a notable liqueur from the United States. It takes its flavour from oranges and from the shaddock, a member of the grape-fruit family.

Glayva is another distinctive Scottish liqueur using whisky as its base.

Goldwasser is an unusual liqueur; tiny gold leaves float about in it, a legacy of the time when gold was widely regarded as a potent means of warding off illness. The liqueur is flavoured with aniseed and caraway.

Grand Marnier is a proprietary brand of curaçao, made in France on a base of Cognac.

Irish Mist Herbs, honey and Irish whiskey are the components of this liqueur from Tullamore in the Irish Republic.

Izarra is a Basque liqueur which has been described unkindly as an attempt to imitate Chartreuse. But it has its individuality. The base is Armagnac, the flavouring herbs, and like Chartreuse it comes in green and yellow, the green being the stronger.

Kahlua is a Mexican contribution to the liqueur spectrum. Its flavouring is coffee.

Kummel is another very popular liqueur featuring grain spirit and caraway seeds. Caraway has a long-standing reputation as an aid to the digestion.

Maraschino Sour cherries are used in the manufacture of this markedly sweet drink. It has an intensely aromatic bouquet and flavour. Among famous brands are Drioli and Luxardo.

Parfait Amour There was a fashion for endowing liqueurs with erotic names. Parfait Amour is a survivor of the trend. It is notable for its brilliant violet hue.

Peach brandy To be exact, peach brandy is the distillate of peaches. But the name is widely used for a liqueur made by macerating fruits with brandy. It has an intense bouquet and is usually very sweet.

Sloe gin Ripe sloe berries are steeped in gin. The best-known brand is Pedlar.

Southern Comfort A big-selling American brand based on Bourbon and using peaches and other fruit in its flavouring.

Strega According to legend, the people who drink this Italian liqueur together will be eternally united; so take care who joins you. It has scores of herbs and barks, is yellow and sweet.

Tia Maria Jamaican rum is the base, and coffee from the Blue Mountains of Jamaica with some spices are the flavourings.

Trappistine is an innocuously light yellow-green coloured liqueur made at the Abbaye de Grâce de Dieu, France. It is based on Armagnac and has herb flavouring.

Van der Hum A strongly orange-flavoured liqueur from South Africa, based on Cape brandy. The name means 'what's-his-name'. Bertrams are the best-known producers.

La Vieille Cure Half a hundred herbs and two kinds of brandy, Cognac and Armagnac, go into this liqueur, made at the abbey of Cenon in France.

Advocaat It is an open question whether this is a liqueur at all. It is certainly unlike any other. The components are eggs and grape brandy. It is usually of fairly low alcoholic strength, and some brands are so thick they need to be supped with a spoon rather than drunk. Advocaat has a reputation as a dependable pick-me-up.

Deep & Cool

Starting a cellar, with the prospect of a dauntingly long and thirsty wait before you at last get to grips with the grimed and cobwebbed bottles, may not sound like the best way of tying up your money. But if your taste is for classic wines, especially those of Bordeaux and Burgundy, or the rare, handsome vintage products of Oporto, there is no more certain hedge against inflation – or, indeed, against famine. A private cache is, moreover, the best means of ensuring that you possess a share of the world's fine wines, for it seems improbable that demand for these precious liquids, which has never been brisker than in the past decade or so, will diminish significantly.

The fact is that too many people want to drink the best, while production cannot be expanded to meet demand if the quality of fine wine is to be maintained.

The 1960s and early 1970s saw a massive surge in the price of quality wines, especially in Bordeaux and Burgundy. The price explosion originated in the excellent vintage of 1961, and it took all of twelve years to burn itself out. In 1969, for example, the price of classed clarets on the Bordeaux market opened forty per cent above the figure for the previous worthwhile vintage, of 1967, while even some of the plainer varieties of claret opened fifty per cent above the 1967 figure. At the Hospices de Beaune sale, watched by the trade as a price barometer for Burgundy, some wines notched up a hundred per cent increase on 1967.

It was a long saga of frantic competitive buying. Companies and individuals making purchases for investment were responsible for setting off the price spiral and for keeping it spiralling once it had begun. They bought wine with no more thought of drinking it than would a philatelist consider sticking his penny black on a letter. Wine had become big money.

By 1973 the market was starting to falter. Some merchants had been flatly refusing to pay the prices demanded in one or two vintages; growers found themselves with full cellars which they were at first reluctant to unload in case things picked up again. But buyers remained thin on the ground. Other merchants offered at auction sales large stocks of fine wines they no longer wanted to afford to keep, and the wine trade waited with bated breath to see whether the bottom was going to drop completely out of the market. That did not happen; fine wine did not become cheap, although it became less dear. A 'wine faking' scandal in Bordeaux was instrumental in depressing the price of generic wines which had also been steadily pushing up in price as they found ready buyers among those who no longer wanted to pay the astronomical prices asked for the better qualities.

All these events have left a rather confused picture as to whether wine hoarding is any longer a worthwhile exercise. It is impossible to make any valid forecast on the future of wine prices. So many speculators have burned their fingers in the culmination of the price explosion, and so much unwanted wine was without buyers for so long, that it seems improbable that the spiral will resume the momentum of 1961–73 in the forseeable future. On the other hand production costs seem certain to go on increasing, so that it is unlikely that quality wines will ever become inexpensive.

The main objective of starting a cellar is to stock it, as far as possible, with bottles that have been bought at the trade's opening price, which is relatively low, and then to wait for it to ripen over the years. By the time it is mature, or nearing maturity, the chances are very high that the same wine, in the same wine merchant's shop, will be offered (if there is any left to offer) at a figure several times higher than the original one.

Appreciation in the value of wine is due to a number of factors. First of all, and most basically, almost *anything* costs money to keep. The wine merchant needs to take account of all his outgoings incurred in keeping a wine: rent, rates, insurance, and so forth. The longer a wine lies in his cellars, the more of these overheads accrue to it.

But external factors have an even more important role to play in determining the eventual price of a wine. Among them are the quality and quantity of subsequent vintages. If, for example, one good vintage is followed by a succession of vintages that are poorly rated, then the good vintage is bound to appreciate fairly dramatically in value. A moderately good vintage can gain in value if the succeeding vintages yield only a low output.

Even in these inflationary times such variations have an impact on the price of fine wine. Bidding can falter if the quantity and quality of a vintage is much the same as last year's. It can rattle up at a breathtaking pace if the vintage shows promise of being 'one of the century's finest', especially if it is short. Every now and then there is a rumour that a vintage is among the best of the century; countless fingers have been burned in the wine markets by this very rumour, and more, no doubt, are waiting to be burned, for there are always those who will not, or don't want to, learn from the lessons of the past.

The private investor in wine has the advantage of being able to observe with detachment the bidding and counter-bidding in the markets of Bordeaux and Beaune. These things are better handled by the wine merchant. His opening prices will take account of his efforts in this area, and no-one will grudge him that. What the private investor gains is the satisfaction of having something to drink in the years ahead that the next man will have to pay through the nose for – if he can get it at all. Or the private investor can, if he chooses, eventually sell, and find satisfaction that way.

Since every vintage is different in some respect from all that have gone before it, so each year's wine is different. Inevitably, then, there are variations in the period that wines from differing years need to lie in bottle before they reach maturity. A vintage that produces fairly light claret will be perhaps only three years old when its harvest is ready for drinking. A heavier claret from a notable vintage may need ten years, or more. Burgundy needs five years on average. Vintage port must have at least ten.

Some dry white wines can improve in bottle over a period of years, and the finest sweet varieties (Sauternes, Tokay, and the best kinds of hock and Moselle) will certainly do so. There is no reason at all why a private cellar should not have a selection of such wines; there is, indeed, every reason why it should, if the collector has a partiality for whites. But in general reds are a great deal more rewarding. They blossom over the years to a peak of perfection; and the cellar owner, when at last he gets his tongue round a mature, superbly-balanced wine, is entitled to feel a glow of paternal satisfaction not just over the wine itself, but over the part, however small it may seem, that he has played in its development. Rosés are not for the long-term cellar. Nor are sparkling wines, with the exception of vintage Champagne, which will go on improving in bottle long after its birth-date.

'Cellar' is no more than a convenience term, for a wine store does not necessarily need to be below ground. It can be in an unused room, in the cupboard-under-the-stairs, or even at the end of the garage. But it is extremely important, if costly fine wines are at stake, that the conditions should be exactly right, for much can go wrong with wine in storage and it is all too easy to see the transformation of a collection of prized bottles into something that has no other future but to be poured away.

The wine store should be fairly dark, free of vibration, clean and well-ventilated. It must have no form of artificial heating. It must not be draughty. It must not be used as a store for things with a pronounced odour, such as paint or floor polish.

The temperature must not show dramatic fluctuations. Ideally it should be maintained at around 10°C. (50°F.).Anything much above this will make the wine mature at an unnaturally rapid rate, so that the best results will not be achieved.

The bottles should be stored on their sides, with the wine in contact with the cork. Otherwise the cork will contract, air will get at the wine, and it will oxidise. The best means of ensuring that the bottles are in the right position is to use plain, utilitarian wine bins, obtainable from most wine merchants, department stores and elsewhere. There are fancy, and usually rather costly, wine bins around these days, so tarted up that they suggest the right place to store wine is in the living room or the dining room, as part of the décor. But these are the wrong places for it, and such bins have no special advantage for serious wine collectors.

At a pinch, segmented wine cases turned on their sides will serve perfectly well as bins, so long as there is plenty of room for the air to circulate round the bottles. Wine merchants are not, today, as open-handed with wooden crates as once they were; most wine cases seem to be made of cardboard. But they have a nasty habit of collapsing after a time, particularly in damp cellars, and the results can be tragic.

Table wines should be laid down with the label uppermost, not only because this helps ready identification, but because, when the wine is taken out, you know that the sediment will always be lying on the reverse side of the bottle. Vintage port bottles may have a white blaze, which should be uppermost.

White wine should be placed nearest to the floor, where it is cooler. Any spirits should stand upright; if they lie flat in bins the liquid will cause the cork to deteriorate after a time. And fortified wines, with the exception of vintage port, should also stand upright.

It sometimes happens that half-bottles, which in the normal course of things are priced at more than half the cost of a full bottle, can be bought at auctions or in merchants' end-of-bin sales for a good deal less than the proportionate full-bottle prices. So half-bottles can be an economical acquisition for the private cellar, but it is important to bear it in mind that wine in halves matures at a faster rate than wine in bottles. Wine in magnums, on the other hand, will mature at a slower rate.

Apart from the bins, a cellar does not need much special equipment. It is useful, however, to keep a cellar-book – a log, as it were, of the progress of the different wines. The question of whether a particular wine really has come along enormously since you opened the first bottle of it nine months ago is much more easily settled if you make a note, when bottles are opened at intervals, of the characteristics of the wines. Such a log will also be of immense help in planning future wine purchases; it will show, for example, the case history of each wine in the cellar – when it was bought, at what price, from whom, when it became drinkable, when it reached its full powers and when it showed signs of going into decline. All this is useful when you come to buy the same sort of wine from a similar vintage, for the book will give a pointer to the differing phases in that wine's career, and to the optimum time for drinking it. In an extensive cellar the book is also valuable as a stock record.

The only other piece of equipment that ought to be in the cellar is the bottle-basket or wine cradle. The cradle is not just a picturesque device for carrying wine to the table, though it is often used for precisely that purpose. In fact, except in the case of an emergency, as when wine has to be brought from the cellar to the table at very short notice, the cradle has no place at the table whatsoever. A wine that needs a cradle is a wine that has sediment, and it follows that such a wine must be decanted.

Transferring a bottle from the bin to the place where it is going to be decanted sounds, on the face of it, a straightforward enough operation. It is important, however, that it should be done with care; any undue motion will stir the sediment into the wine, with the result that it will be unfit to drink until the sediment has settled. In an old, heavily sedimented red, this could take as much as forty-eight hours.

It is perfectly possible to perform this transfer operation without the assistance of a cradle, but there is no doubt that a cradle makes matters simpler. You ease the bottle, in its horizontal position, out of its niche in the bin and into the cradle, which is so constructed as to allow the bottle to remain horizontal while it is carried from the cellar to the place of decanting. Then you gently ease out the cork and decant, with patience. The wine will pour clear and bright, while the sediment will gradually slide down the inside of the bottle and gather near the bottom of it.

A private cellar, even on a fairly modest scale, can give immense pleasure. The limitation for most people is space. Every nook and cranny of the modern house is allocated to some specific purpose; wine storage is not one of them. And even in houses which do have a spare cupboard or an accessible attic, there are often problems because, for example, the cupboard has hot water pipes running through it or the attic has a very variable temperature.

In such circumstances you do not need to be deprived of the fascination of selecting and controlling your own private hoard of wines. You do not even need to have a house at all. Many of the major wine merchants, and some smaller ones too, will store your wines in their own cellars. They will make sure that the storage conditions are as they should be (after all, a lot of their own valuable stock will be lying in the same cellar) and some will send you a report from time to time on how the wine is coming on.

This service is not, of course, free of charge, but the outgoings, which should include not only rental for the space occupied but insurance cover, are seldom formidable. With inflation rattling away in Bordeaux and elsewhere, it seems more than likely that your cache of wine will show a comforting rate of appreciation even after taking account of the outgoings.

It would be presumptuous to offer advice on the kind of wines that should be selected for a cellar. The choice is very much a matter of personal taste, and its nature is dictated by the availability of hard cash. It is dependant, too, on what is on the market at any given time. But it seems sensible, in making the selection, to avoid restricting it to wines that are not going to attain maturity for a long period of years. These should be there, of course, if you have the patience to wait for them, but there should also be wines which, even if they come from a notable vintage, are going to be at the peak of their development before the great wines of such a vintage. In Bordeaux, for instance, the top growths in a great vintage can take many years to mature; they begin life as hard, bitter liquid that is scarcely drinkable. Only time can work its magic to make them smooth-textured and mellow. But many lesser growths are meeker from the outset; they do not need so long in bottle, and may, indeed, start going downhill if they are unopened for too many years. Many clarets from the famous 1961 vintage will not be poured until well into the 1980s; but a multitude of their lesser kinsmen have long since been ready for drinking, and have been drunk.

A cellar should, therefore, include a selection of these lesser wines, whether from good vintages or from vintages of moderate quality. The ideal strategy for a cellar is to have at least one variety that will be ready for drinking in every year for the next ten or fifteen.

Also in the cellar should be some wines that are ready now, and others that will be ready within the next year or two – wines, in short, for current drinking. This has the simple attraction of affording the facility of having wine 'on tap', as it were. The man with such wines in his cellar is not hamstrung by shop closing hours. He is prepared when guests turn up at short notice. He can help himself to a bottle on a whim, instead of having to plan ahead.

For this purpose, choose (unless you have decided personal likes and dislikes) a reasonable variety of wines, taking in red, white and rosé, dry, medium and sweet. Then there is something on hand for any occasion from a formal three- or four-course dinner to a simple supper dish like pasta. Many whites and rosés are also useful as aperitifs.

Some of the wines in this current drinking cache can be simple, everyday bottles; others, if the store is to be a comprehensive one that can provide the wines for a formal dinner, obviously need to be more stylish. But they should all have the same treatment, being stored on their sides and, except in the case of the plainest kinds, which are intended for more or less immediate consumption, handled with respect. Take care not to let the plainer varieties, especially whites, lie in the cellar for more than six months. Even cheap wines can improve in bottle, but there is a risk that, instead of improving, they will fade.

One fruitful ground for the wine hunter is the saleroom. Various auctioneers hold wine sales from time to time, the most notable people in the business being such London firms as Christie's and Sotheby's. Many wines are sold without a reserve price or else with a very low one. Much wine changes hands at figures well below current trade prices.

Auctioneers generally extend the same facilities to the modest, first-time buyer as they do to the regular big spender. You are, for example, welcome at the pre-sale tasting. Sellers are encouraged to provide a sample of each wine on offer, with the exception of what Christie's describe as 'wines of unassailable repute' – famous vintages of château-bottled claret, for example, or very rare wines. These apart, the intending buyer may taste what he chooses, although as Sotheby's put it: 'If we spot someone coming regularly for a kind of cocktail party and never buying, we politely tell him we'd rather not see him again.'

If, having found your wine in the catalogue, you have not the slightest idea of what you ought to offer for it, the auctioneer will advise. He knows his world wine market and has a pretty good idea of the price each lot is likely to fetch.

He will also, if you are unable to attend the sale in person, bid on your behalf. All you need to do is write, giving the lot number and your maximum bid. Alternative lots can be specified.

The wine auction bidder has few 'extras' to pay. The catalogue costs a nominal sum. You may be asked to pay for the packing and carriage of your purchase, but this will be kept to a minimum and it is, in any case, an outgoing you are quite likely to meet if you require a wine merchant to pack and deliver. Unless your purchase is remarkably cheap it will be worth taking out insurance to augment the carrier's limited liability for losses or breakages.

Not surprisingly, auctioneers are not keen to discuss specific areas for potential bargains. Their job, after all, is to get the best possible price for the vendor. Moreover, trends change and will continue to change; today's bargain could be pricy tomorrow.

Obviously, however, salerooms are not a source of cut-price bottles among rare and fine wines. These have an established market value, and prices are much more likely to find that value, or move above it, than to fall below. Thus if the man who paid £220 at Christie's for a bottle of 1811 Tokay Essenz has drunk it and needs a replacement, the chances are that he will have to fork out more than that figure.

It is among wines of lesser fame that the bargain bottles are to be found. Sales of surplus stock or cellar clearances are likely to be a rich vein of bottles of good, middle-class wines, just waiting to be snapped up at prices that would make your wine merchant wince. And if you stick to half-bottles you have every prospect of coming away with an economical bag of prized clarets; there is not a great deal of interest in half-bottles at auctions, and the more famous their name, the less the interest is.

Many people, and particularly those with a cellar, consider buying wine as a commercial investment – buying, that is, with the express intention of reselling at some future date in the hope of making a profit. This is certainly possible, but it is full of pitfalls, and it is by no means inconceivable that the hoped-for profit will turn out to be a loss.

The practice makes some people in the wine trade rather unhappy (wine, they say, is for drinking, not for money-making) and there is some measure of feeling against the speculators whose activities pushed up prices in Bordeaux and Burgundy. Nevertheless there are no rules against speculative buying, but you need to be prepared to spend fairly freely if your money is to show a worthwhile return. Small-scale investment is scarcely worth the trouble.

If, for example, a parcel of highly-rated Burgundy were to double in value over two or three years, the total gain on it will not be nearly as handsome as it appears to be. You will need to insure it. You will need (unless you have your own cellar – but home-kept wines are likely to be regarded with dubiety by potential purchasers) to pay a wine merchant to store it for you. And when you take it to the saleroom you will need to pay the auctioneer's commission.

On top of all that there is the agonising risk that something will go wrong with the wine between purchase and resale. Then your investment is worth zero.

There is money to be made, despite all these drawbacks, but you must buy shrewdly and on a significant scale, preferably with the advice of a wine merchant or broker. Otherwise your money would be better off kept on deposit in the bank.

Menus

Menu One

Crab soufflé
*An austere white such as Chablis,
Soave or Muscadet*

Pheasant with nut stuffing
Game chips
Braised celery
Brussels sprouts
*Pheasant is light for game so choose a
light-flavoured red like Volnay or a good claret.*

Cheese and biscuits

Fresh pineapple

Menu Two

Smoked fish pâté
*Any inexpensive hock or other dry Riesling,
or dry white Bordeaux*

Coq au vin
Creamy mashed potatoes
Green beans with sage
*Preferably the wine used in the preparation of
the coq au vin, but certainly not an inferior wine*

Cheese and biscuits

Danish apple cake
*A modest Sauternes or chilled dessert wine
like Bual, Malmsey or Samos*

Menu Three

Cold watercress soup

Poached salmon
Hollandaise sauce
New potatoes
Minted peas
*Any white that is sufficiently fruity to stand up
to the sauce – Chassagne-Montrachet, Meursault or
Gewürztraminer are all good candidates. Poached
salmon can also accommodate a chilled light red
like Beaujolais or Valpolicella.*

Fresh raspberries or strawberries with cream

Winter Buffet

Onion quiche
Goulash
Rice or noodles
Sautéed mushrooms

Syllabub

*This needs a rich red. Hungarian Bull's Blood
fits the bill nicely and economically. More
upstage, but still moderately priced, is
Châteauneuf-du-Pape or a modest red Burgundy.*

Menu Four

Cream of celery soup

Lamb, green pepper and mushroom brochettes
Saffron rice
Grilled tomatoes
*A middleweight claret would be admirable; either
Chianti or a red Rioja would make very
acceptable alternatives.*

Cheese and biscuits

Caramel oranges

Menu Five

Avocado vinaigrette

Boeuf à la bourguignonne
New potatoes with parsley
French beans
*Pommard or Nuits-Saint-Georges. Cheaper wines
can be used in the preparation of this stew.*

Cheese and biscuits

Zabaglione
*A glass of Marsala, perhaps, but the dish is
rich enough already.*

Menu Six

Smoked haddock mousse
*An inexpensive Riesling or a branded
white Burgundy*

Escalopes of turkey breast garnished with lemon
New potatoes with parsley
Asparagus
Green salad
*A white or a red will be equally agreeable.
The white could be Moselle or Vouvray, the red Mâcon or
Beaujolais Villages.*

Cheese and biscuits

Fresh fruit salad and cream

Summer Buffet

Ham bouchées
Assorted canapés
Cold salmon mayonnaise
Salads, various

Vacherin

*Choose a selection of adaptable wines, with a
lightweight red, a full white and a sturdy rosé.
Examples are Zinfandel, Alsatian Riesling and
Provençal rosé.*

Index

Acknowledgements

The colour photographs in this book were taken by the following:
A. Bernhaut, by courtesy of PAF International page 112
John Bradshaw page 35
Iain Erskine, by courtesy of Moët & Chandon page 129 top and bottom right
Michael Kuh, by courtesy of Pedro Domecq, S. A. page 140 top left
Colin Maher pages 67, 71, 74, 75, 78, 79, 81, 84, 85, 105 top, 113 top right, 155 left
Peter Titmuss jacket, pages 38 bottom, 39, 42, 43, 46, 47, 49, 56, 57, 60, 61, 64, 101, 104, 105 bottom, 125, 129 left, 133

The black and white photographs were taken by the following:
Iain Erskine, by courtesy of Moët & Chandon pages 130, 131
Michael Kuh, by courtesy of Pedro Domecq, S.A. page 149
Joseph McKenzie, by courtesy of The Glenlivet Distillers Limited pages 152, 157
Colin Maher pages 69, 72, 73, 77, 82, 83, 87
Peter Titmuss page 135

The author and publishers would like to thank the following for their help in providing photographs for the book:

Colour photographs
Croft & Ca. Lda. pages 140 top right, 141
Pedro Domecq, S.A. pages 137, 144, 146, 147
Food from France pages 52, 53

Gilbey S.A. page 38 top
Grants of St. James's pages 89, 92, 96, 97
IPC Books Pty Limited page 120
Justerini & Brooks Limited pages 151, 155 top right
House of Martell, Cognac page 154
South African Wine Farmers Association Limited page 121 top left
Teltscher Brothers Limited pages 109, 113 bottom
Wine Institute, San Francisco pages 117, 121 top right and bottom

Black and white photographs
Croft & Ca. Lda. page 139
Delaforce Sons & Ca. pages 142, 148
Kiola S.p.A. page 99
Piat Père et Fils S.A. pages 45, 59

Many other people have helped in numerous ways with the preparation of this book. In particular we should like to thank:
The Embassy of the Argentine Republic
Bordeaux Direct
The Brazilian Embassy
Buckingham Vintners International Limited
Embajada de Chile
Henry Clark of International Distillers and Vintners Export Limited
Fromm and Sichel Inc.
M. Manoncourt of Château Figeac, Saint-Emilion
Robin Young of James Murray (Glasgow) Limited